Contents

■

Acknowledgements

Introduction

Part I MANAGING CUSTOMER LOYALTY

1 The importance of customer loyalty   2

2 Allocating responsibility for customer loyalty   17

3 Identifying opportunities   35

4 Taking the initiative   46

5 Building staff commitment and understanding   52

6 Raising customer awareness   62

7 Providing staff with skills   69

8 Building partnership   73

Part II CUSTOMER LOYALTY IN ACTION

9 Winning with service   80

10 The oil business   103

11 Components suppliers   111

12 Travel agent programmes   127

13 Delivering consultancy services   139

14 Information systems   153

15 Retaining customer loyalty in a car dealership   161

16 Financial institutions   178

17 Developing loyalty in the retail sector   193

18 Conclusion   205

   Index   207

Acknowledgements

∎

Many people have helped to bring this book to publication, particularly Jonathan Glasspool at BIM and David Crosby, publisher at Pitman. I would like to thank them for their encouragement and guidance. A number of professional colleagues have contributed indirectly by allowing me to work with them on customer loyalty projects; they include: Vic Cripps, Stuart Flanagan, Steve Morton, Roger Burrell, Derek Lamb, Chris Swafflin-Smith, Dr Nick Georgiades, Jack Fearnside, Charles Peile, John Latham and Susan Young, Finally, I would like to thank my wife Dorreen and my children Sarah and John for their patience in living through another book.

Building
Customer
Loyalty

■

Building Customer Loyalty

■

IAN LINTON

*i**n*** the Institute
of Management

PITMAN PUBLISHING

The Institute of Management (IM) is at the forefront of management development and best management practice. The Institute embraces all levels of management from students to chief executives. It provides a unique portfolio of services for all managers, enabling them to develop skills and achieve management excellence. If you would like to hear more about the benefits of membership, please write to Department P, Institute of Management, Cottingham Road, Corby NN17 1TT. This series is commissioned by the Institute of Management Foundation.

Pitman Publishing
128 Long Acre, London WC2E 9AN

A Division of Longman Group UK Limited

First published in 1993

© Ian Linton 1993

A CIP catalogue record for this book can be obtained
from the British Library.

ISBN 0 273 60080 X

Photoset in Linotron Century Schoolbook by
Northern Phototypesetting Co., Ltd., Bolton.
Printed and bound by Bell and Bain Ltd., Glasgow

Introduction

∎

Customer loyalty is one of the most important issues facing businesses today. Unless companies can retain the loyalty of their customers, they will not be able to ensure repeat business and their long-term future will be uncertain.

Companies who sell products with a short sales cycle – food or newspapers, for example – can use short-term promotional techniques to stimulate repeat purchase. However, companies with a longer sales cycle – cars or computers, for example – have to maintain contact and build loyalty over a much longer period of time.

This book explains why customer loyalty is an important issue for every business and, more important, why it is a challenge facing every manager. Customer loyalty is everyone's responsibility.

Building Customer Loyalty is divided into two main parts – the first part describes the importance of customer loyalty and the management actions needed to support it. The second part looks at customer loyalty programmes in action in a variety of different market sectors. The examples are not, however, intended to be specific to just that sector; they illustrate general approaches which can be applied to many different markets.

Scope of the book

THE IMPORTANCE OF CUSTOMER LOYALTY

Building customer loyalty is not an isolated task; it is an integral part of managing every business. Operating customer loyalty programmes will have a significant impact on your long-term business prospects and will influence many of the other management actions that you and your team take. This opening chapter shows how you should review your business in the light of the following activities:

- improving long-term business performance;
- influencing product development;

- focusing the organisation on the customer;
- ensuring repeat purchase;
- increasing customer retention;
- shortening purchase cycles;
- enhancing the ownership experience;
- managing customer relationships;
- opening sales channels;
- controlling sales costs;
- contributing to long-term planning; and
- dealing with competitive activity.

ALLOCATING RESPONSIBILITY FOR CUSTOMER LOYALTY

Building customer loyalty is everyone's responsibility. However, many departments within a company do not have direct contact with customers and feel that they cannot contribute to customer loyalty. This chapter looks at the potential contribution of each of the following departments:

- sales;
- distribution;
- manufacturing;
- purchasing;
- design and development;
- marketing;
- communications;
- personnel;
- training;
- customer service;
- administration;
- quality; and
- service.

IDENTIFYING OPPORTUNITIES

Every business must take positive action to build customer loyalty. Before that process begins, it is important to be aware of the actions that can have the greatest impact on customer loyalty. This chapter describes how to identify opportunities in your company by:

- developing a planned after-care programme to maintain contact after the sale;
- providing services which your customers need to make effective use of your products;

- offering a total business solution so that your customers depend on you as a single source of supply;

- analysing complaints and taking corrective action so that you can overcome problems, rather than lose customers;

- carrying out research into customers' needs;

- operating customer surveys so that customers have a clearly defined route for consultation;

- monitoring competitive activity to see where you can make further improvements;

- adding value to your products so that you differentiate your products from the competition; and

- analysing your customers' business life cycles so that you can identify opportunities to provide relevant products or services.

TAKING THE INITIATIVE

Customer loyalty programmes must be driven. Without a strong sense of direction and urgency, they will drift and staff will lose interest after an initial burst of enthusiasm. This chapter explains how managers can introduce customer loyalty programmes and maintain the momentum by:

- making customer loyalty a priority so that everyone in the organisation is aware of its importance;

- getting top-level commitment to ensure that the programmes have adequate funding and resources;

- setting standards so that staff understand what they have to achieve to build customer loyalty;

- ranking customer requirements to ensure that the company's resources are concentrated on the most productive tasks;

- setting key performance objectives as a basis for training and funding;

- identifying opportunities for improvement and responding to research and customer feedback;

- issuing a statement of direction to ensure that future developments are in line with the customer loyalty strategy; and

- allocating responsibility for managing the programme and individual activities.

BUILDING STAFF COMMITMENT AND UNDERSTANDING

Building staff commitment and understanding is an essential part of the customer loyalty process. This chapter explains how to develop the highest levels of commitment by:

- creating a customer focused environment to maximise the skills of your staff;
- auditing staff understanding to identify awareness and plan customer loyalty communications;
- demonstrating individual contribution to show staff why their actions matter;
- identifying customer expectations so that people are directly aware of the impact of their actions;
- targeting key staff to get the highest performance from staff with the greatest impact on customer loyalty;
- introducing recognition and reward to motivate staff to achieve the highest standards of customer service; and
- reporting progress to maintain the impetus of customer loyalty programmes.

RAISING CUSTOMER AWARENESS

Although customer loyalty programmes should demonstrate to customers that you are a caring organisation, you can reinforce the benefits of the programmes by operating a positive customer communications programme. This chapter explains the key elements of this:

- developing a contact strategy to maintain effective planned contact with customers;
- optimising customer contact by making sure that every form of contact creates the right impression and builds loyalty;
- carrying out customer consultation to get involved in your customers' business;
- managing complaints to demonstrate that you care about your customers' concerns;
- carrying out customer satisfaction surveys to measure satisfaction and build two-way communications;

- making the most of direct mail to maintain regular contact with targeted customers; and
- integrating customer loyalty into all your communications.

PROVIDING STAFF WITH SKILLS

Staff training is an essential part of the customer loyalty process – ensuring that staff have the skills to make an effective contribution. This chapter explains how the process could be managed by:

- defining staff contribution and measuring their performance against customer loyalty standards;
- identifying training needs to ensure that it is focused on critical areas;
- integrating training with customer care to develop personal skills that will build customer loyalty; and
- improving management skills to ensure that customer loyalty is effectively managed.

BUILDING PARTNERSHIP

Partnership is an extreme form of customer loyalty in which customer and supplier work closely together to achieve mutual benefits such as security of supply and continuity of contact. To build and maintain partnership takes a sustained management effort to:

- identify partnership opportunities by analysing your customers' business activities;
- understand and develop the changing relationships between customer and supplier through a continuous communications programme;
- change sales force attitudes to ensure they build relationships rather than just sell products;
- manage account relationships so that customers recognise partnership as essential to their business success;
- use services to maintain contact and add value;
- add value by enhancing your customers' skills; and
- meet customers' changing requirements by working closely with the customer team.

WINNING WITH SERVICE

The service sector demonstrates how services can be used to build customer loyalty. It also shows that services can be differentiated in a number of ways to add value to customer relationships and reduce the impact of competition. The key actions include:

- supporting your customers' business with service so that they depend on you;
- providing customers with a single source of service to simplify their administration, offer consistency and quality and strengthen relationships;
- integrating your service with a customer's business to differentiate a commodity service and increase dependence;
- introducing higher standards of service to maintain an edge over price competitors;
- improving the response to service queries to make it easier for customers to buy from you;
- maintaining customer relationships with long-term service plans;
- matching the level of service to your customers' needs to segment the market and improve customer relationships; and
- improving convenience for customers to demonstrate the highest levels of customer care.

THE OIL BUSINESS

Oil is a commodity product which competes with other forms of energy such as gas and electricity. The oil companies also compete with each other to secure long-term contracts and they use the quality of service to differentiate their offer. This service is based on helping their customers get the best from oil products and includes the following activities:

- providing contract research to customers as a means of getting involved in the customer's future plans and improving relationships;
- providing technical support to customers so that they rely on your technical expertise;
- offering customers your core skills to help them set up or manage activities that are crucial to their own success; and
- helping your customers manage their operations by providing them with access to your operating information and management skills.

COMPONENTS SUPPLIERS

The components market is highly fragmented with fierce price competition and little opportunity for product differentiation. The strategies include:

- providing service support to customers to improve their own skills and provide a better overall service;
- branding commodity products to differentiate them from the competition;
- providing customers with their own range of branded components so that they can provide a quality service to their own ultimate customers;
- helping your customers reduce costs by working in partnership with their design team;
- building confidence through quality;
- improving delivery times to demonstrate customer care;
- using technical consultancy to build partnership; and
- providing customers with an efficient local service by supporting distributors.

TRAVEL AGENT PROGRAMMES

Success in the travel industry, like many other businesses depends on understanding customers' needs and developing the skills and products to meet those needs. The key management activities include:

- improving standards of customer service in retail outlets;
- improving the quality of customer information to enhance high standards of personal service;
- packaging services for specific market sectors so that they reflect customers' real needs;
- building the loyalty of distributors by supporting their business operations;
- demonstrating the quality of service by operating a highly visible customer care programme; and
- maintaining contact with customers through planned direct marketing programmes.

DELIVERING CONSULTANCY SERVICES

Professional services are often delivered as a series of one-off projects with no guarantee of continuity of work. Yet both customer and consultancy could benefit from a continuing relationship. This chapter describes a number of techniques for building stronger relationships:

- increasing contact through complete business solutions which support your core activities;

- improving your customers' management skills and helping them to enhance their own performance;

- working with your customers' management teams so that you get involved in the development of their business;

- developing your customers' staff so that you build higher levels of customer satisfaction;

- extending consultancy into implementation and maintenance to increase the level of customer contact and account control;

- using programme management to strengthen customer relationships; and

- widening a consultancy discipline to increase the level of customer contact.

INFORMATION SYSTEMS

Computer companies have followed the lead of professional service organisations and used services to build loyalty. The sales cycle for information systems is long and it is vital that suppliers maintain contact between sales. This chapter describes the strategy which includes:

- providing a business solution which helps customers achieve the best return on their investment in computer systems;

- adding value to computer systems by helping customers improve their own business performance;

- focusing on your customers' markets so that services reflect the specialist needs of different market sectors; and

- offering customers your core services so that you add further value to the relationship.

RETAINING CUSTOMER LOYALTY IN A CAR DEALERSHIP

Customers rarely change their cars until the second or third year of ownership and that makes it difficult for manufacturers and dealers to maintain effective contact between sales. Car manufacturers have led the way in operating customer loyalty programmes, and this chapter shows examples of their approach:

■ making the most of parts and service operations to attract customers to the dealership;

■ introducing retailing techniques to a supply business to increase the level of contact;

■ improving convenience for customers to build higher levels of satisfaction;

■ winning back lost service customers by running a series of loyalty-building promotional offers;

■ supporting volume customers through distributors by offering service and management support;

■ supporting business users by offering them higher levels of convenience; and

■ operating community programmes to increase the opportunity for informal contact.

FINANCIAL INSTITUTIONS

Financial institutions have an opportunity to build 'customers for life'. By analysing their customers' changing needs, they can develop a range of products and services that continue to meet those changing needs. This chapter gives an example of how a combination of product development and personal service was helping to achieve this. The techniques included:

■ operating 'customers for life' programmes;

■ using card marketing to segment the market and maintain customer loyalty at a number of different levels;

■ offering customers greater choice and packaging services to appeal to specific groups of customers;

■ increasing customer convenience by using appropriate new technology;

- providing support for small businesses by improving the quality of advice and improving standards of service;

- matching financial services to customers' needs to increase dependence;

- giving customers the benefits of your technology to build stronger relationships; and

- helping customers build international business by offering your experience and skills.

DEVELOPING LOYALTY IN THE RETAIL SECTOR

In the retail sector, the quality of personal service makes a major contribution to building customer satisfaction and loyalty. However, there are many other factors which can be used to retain customers. This chapter describes a number of techniques, including:

- improving the quality of staff by providing training and sales support;

- improving product information so that customers find it easier to buy from you;

- focusing facilities on the customer to attract customers;

- giving customers greater choice by introducing new products and facilities;

- using card marketing to build customer information and reward loyalty; and

- building customer loyalty at the point of sale by using sales promotion techniques to encourage repeat purchase.

These techniques can be used by any company that sells its products through retail outlets.

Part I

■

MANAGING CUSTOMER LOYALTY

1

The importance of customer loyalty

'Against a background of greatly increased customer expectations and increasing difficulty in sustaining product advantages, how can a manufacturer distinguish itself from the competition in the longer term? How can it build and maintain brand loyalty?'

This quotation from a presentation to automotive manu-facturers highlights an issue that faces just about every company that sells products and services to consumers or business. The presenter's response sums up one approach.

'The answer lies in delivering the quality of aftermarket service which the modern consumer expects and demands. A vehicle can't be sold in isolation – it must be part of a total package of comfort, convenience, value and reliability throughout the ownership cycle. Research shows that a customer satisfied with after-sales service is three times more likely to buy another car from us than a dissatisfied customer.'

There are some important phrases here:

- quality of service;
- total package of comfort, convenience;
- satisfied customers;
- modern consumers expect and demand; and
- throughout the ownership cycle.

They show that to build customer loyalty, a manufacturer must concentrate on customers' needs.

'The consumer has changed . . . a consumer who has become better informed and more discerning. He recognises and expects excellence.

The successful manufacturers are those that have recognised these changes in the consumer. They listen to and understand his needs and are taking steps to meet his expectations. If they can do that, the manufacturer can look forward to increased long-term market share as a result of satisfied customers repurchasing his products. And the consumer can rest in the knowledge that when he buys, he isn't just buying a machine, he is buying a complete service of after care which will last the life of the product.'*

In case anyone doubts the importance of customer loyalty and its implications for long-term business performance, here's a further extract from that automotive industry presentation.

'The world value of the parts and service market for cars is, at a conservative estimate, $100 billion a year. This statistic underlines the fact that the automotive industry, as well as being one of the world's major manufacturing industries, is also one of the largest service industries in the world. After-sales service has become one of the most important factors of all in determining competitive vehicle market shares and the overall success of vehicle manufacturers.'

It is important that you and your management team understand the implications for your business. Unless you understand what you are trying to achieve, customer loyalty activities will be carried out in isolation – they are in fact an integral part of business activity. This introductory chapter outlines some of the customer loyalty activities and implications you should review. They include:

- improving long-term business performance;
- influencing product development;
- focusing the organisation on the customer;
- ensuring repeat purchase;
- increasing customer retention;
- shortening purchase cycles;
- enhancing the ownership experience;
- managing customer relationships;

*For convenience, the personal pronoun 'he' has been used here and throughout the book.

3

- opening sales channels;
- controlling sales costs;
- contributing to long-term planning;
- dealing with competitive activity.

Improving long-term business performance

Does your business have a long-term focus?
What are your long-term objectives?
Do you know who your customers will be in 1 year, 3 years or 5 years?
What actions should you take to improve your long-term performance?

4

'Today's consumer is better informed, more discerning and more insistent on quality and service. This can work to our advantage as long as we can meet their needs more efficiently and cost-effectively than our competitors. If we can do that, we can look forward to increased long-term market share as a result of customers repurchasing our products.'

The net effect of customer loyalty is improved long-term business performance and that, in turn, provides a firm basis for planning, developing new products, and investing in the business. It's this dependence on long-term performance that drives companies to set strategic targets that are customer-focused. The following is an example of a customer-driven target:

To be a low-cost producer of the highest quality products and services which provide the best customer value.

This translates easily into the following long-term philosophy.

Quality is defined by the customer; the customer wants products and services that, throughout their lives, meet his or her needs and expectations at a cost that represents value.

The key phrase is 'throughout their lives' because 'retaining customers for life' is the key to long-term profitability. Here are some actions that businesses have taken to achieve that objective:

- work towards an attitude of continuous improvement;
- stress quality over the life of the product;
- improve research before, during and after delivery;
- invest in training to ensure the right skills are in position at all times;
- maintain continuous process reviews; and
- improve ability to measure quality from customer perspectives.

ACTION

▶ **Look at your own business to see which of these activities will have the greatest impact on your long-term performance.**

▶ **Make a list of priority actions and review these with your colleagues.**

▶ **Use the action programmes for this book that are appropriate to your business.**

5

Influencing product development

What does the level of repeat purchase say about your products and services?

How can you use information about customer satisfaction in your product development programmes?

What impact will new product plans have on customer loyalty?

A business with loyal customers has demonstrated that it understands customer needs. Analysing the way customers buy products through customer satisfaction surveys and other forms of customer research gives important clues to the development of new products and services.

- *Is there a long gap between purchases?*
  The emphasis could be on the development of services to maintain contact between purchases and add value to the product.
- *Are certain aspects of the product causing dissatisfaction?*

The emphasis must be on product improvement.

■ *Are customers looking for greater choice?*
The emphasis could be on adding new products to the range. However, the new products should meet a set of criteria which research has shown are important to customer loyalty.

The best companies consult their customers about new products. One company issues quarterly bulletins to its customers on its research and development programme. Before it launches a new product, the company goes through a consultation programme – advising customers of the broad direction of the new product, inviting comments and then building in customer-driven modifications where they are practical.

ACTION

► **Review all the customer research material available.**
► **Check it against the product development programme to see that new products reflect customer needs.**
► **Consult your customers about new product developments.**

6

Focusing the organisation on the customer

Do you know who is responsible for customer loyalty in your business?
Who should be involved in customer loyalty activities?
How can you make people more aware of their responsibilities?

'Listen to both our internal and external customers, know their wants and needs, and respond to those needs with products and services more quickly than the competition.'

Customer loyalty programmes help to focus an organisation on its customers, but it is important that the philosophy is turned into action.

'We should be the best at knowing our customers and we should *take actions that show we are customer-driven. We should champion customer-oriented training and career development and reward customer-oriented employees.'*

The problem with customer care programmes is that everyone thinks it's someone else's responsibility. A customer loyalty programme with a high profile can change all that by focusing people inside the organisation on the customer's needs. The programme should relate customer concerns directly to the people who caused the problem.

- Mechanics who see themselves as remote from the customer are told about grease marks on the steering wheel.
- Warehouse staff are told about the frustration of parts that are not available when they're promised.
- Receptionists find out about the phone calls that were not returned and inspectors about the niggling fault that wasn't cured.

Building customer loyalty is everyone's responsibility and a programme should be wide-ranging enough to focus everyone's attention on it.

ACTION

- ▶ **Use the checklists later in the book to identify the key staff responsible for customer loyalty.**
- ▶ **Make sure they are aware of their responsibilities.**
- ▶ **Ensure that everyone else in the business understands the importance and practical implications of customer loyalty.**

Ensuring repeat purchase

What percentage of your business comes from repeat purchase?

How important is repeat business to your organisation?

How can customer loyalty programmes influence levels of repeat purchase?

Repeat business is the lifeblood of any company and a high percentage of business comes from a small number of customers. The rule that 80 per cent of a company's business comes from 20 per cent of its customers demonstrates the power of repeat business and customer loyalty. The cost of winning new customers can be high, but repeat business can often be won when customers are satisfied with the product or service.

That means that a company needs to protect its regular customers to ensure long-term stability, yet few companies have a planned programme for attracting repeat business. While there are excellent examples of special offers and promotional activities to stimulate re-purchase, many are based on a short-term ad hoc approach and are not balanced with other activities which can build loyalty.

- Money off next purchase does not add value or differentiate the product from competitors.
- Promotional offers may be irrelevant to the product's brand values.

ACTION

- ► **Look closely at your customer base to identify your most loyal customers.**
- ► **Look at the potential among other customers.**
- ► **Check your current promotions to see whether they build long-term loyalty or short-term sales.**

Increasing customer retention

Are you retaining customers or just increasing product sales?

Could you sell different services or products to your customers to strengthen their loyalty?

Are there any other business actions you can take to retain customers?

Customer retention is closely linked to repeat purchase, but has different aims – repeat purchase programmes are built around products rather than customers. Customer loyalty programmes, on the other hand, focus on the real and changing needs of customers so that the organisation is driven by customers and not by products.

Processes like consultation, customer dialogue, feedback, customer focus are all powerful tools to ensure that companies are listening to what their customers want. If the company does not supply products or services that meet those needs, then the company should be developing these or sourcing them from somewhere else so that they can provide the customer with the solution they want.

ACTION

► **Analyse the purchasing patterns of your major customers.**
► **Research your customers' real needs.**
► **Identify opportunities for selling other products or services.**

Shortening purchase cycles

How frequently do customers buy from you?

Is the gap between purchases too large to maintain regular contact?

Does the purchase cycle provide opportunities to sell other products or services?

The term 'purchase cycle' is used to describe the interval between purchases. For certain food items, the purchasing cycle may be weekly or even daily, but higher value goods such as cars or refrigerators have a purchasing cycle that lasts several years. Cars for example are replaced every two to three years, while domestic electrical products may be replaced every five years or even longer. In business-to-business marketing the purchase cycle for capital purchases of major equipment such as new office equipment or information systems can be at least five years or longer.

The gap between purchases is a dangerous time when customers can forget about your company and competitors can make inroads on your business. Customer loyalty programmes increase the level of contact between an organisation and its customers, and quality contact can be the vital factor in retaining those customers.

Here are some examples of maintaining contact after the sale:

- customer surveys to see if they are satisfied with the product;
- repair and maintenance services; and
- special offers to established customers.

The purchasing cycle can also be analysed to identify other opportunities for introducing new products and services. Chapter 3 (Identifying opportunities) describes this in more detail.

ACTION

▶ **Analyse the purchasing cycles for your main products and services.**

▶ **Identify opportunities for contact between purchases.**

▶ **Look for additional sales opportunities.**

Enhancing the ownership experience

Do your customers get more than just a product when they buy from you?
Are you 'adding value' to your products?
Are you delivering customer satisfaction throughout the ownership period?

'Customers don't just buy a product, they buy a package of the product, service and care before and after delivery of the product.'

Owning a product must be a memorable experience at all levels – not just at the point of purchase, but throughout the period of ownership. This is what helps to build customer satisfaction and is an essential element in achieving customer loyalty.

Satisfying the customer throughout the period of ownership adds value to a product and helps to differentiate it from competitors. It ensures the right level of contact between product purchases and may also provide incremental income from the sale of additional products and services.

ACTION

► **Identify the stages in the ownership experience where it is possible to add value.**

► **Look at competitive activities to see how products and services can be differentiated.**

Managing customer relationships

Have your sales force got control over their main accounts?
Do you have the opportunity to demonstrate customer care?
Would you like to increase the level of contact on your main accounts?

In business-to-business marketing, account relationships are the key to long-term success. Customer loyalty programmes give the sales force the opportunity to contact their customers at regular intervals to maintain the right level of control. This contact is important because it keeps the sales force close to the customer – ensuring that they are aware of any competitive activity and helping them to keep up to date with the customer's changing business requirements.

Regular contact is essential when there is a long time between major purchases – it provides the opportunity to demonstrate customer care and to take a proactive response to customer relations. Many information systems companies, for example, have introduced a broad range of customer services to ensure that they are in regular contact and can provide the highest level of care.

ACTION

▶ **Assess the current level of contact on your major accounts.**

▶ **Review opportunities for improved contact through customer loyalty programmes.**

Opening sales channels

Are you selling a full range of products and services to your customers?
Have you got a plan for meeting customers' changing needs?
Are there opportunities to sell additional products and services?

Customer loyalty programmes encourage repeat purchase and they also provide a valuable channel for selling additional products and services. For example, companies who sell consumer durable products have an immediate opportunity to sell parts, service and accessories over an extended period. And, if they diversify their product range, they can offer new products and services to the same customers. The concept of 'customers for life' is a logical conclusion to customer loyalty programmes.

Banks, for example, have comprehensive data on their customers. People rarely change bank accounts, yet their financial circumstances change over a period of time – an ideal opportunity for meeting changing customer needs. Looking at a bank customer from a very early age, the range of services could include junior savings account, student banking services and loans, bank account services for the first job, mortgage and personal loans for home-buying. Later the focus could change to insurance and savings schemes, personal pensions, loans for car purchase or home improvement. When the customers are older and more prosperous, they may need investment advice and more sophisticated savings schemes, together with a broader range of financial services.

However, unless the bank treats them as customers for life and looks at their business with a degree of continuity, they will lose the incremental business opportunities to other financial organisations.

Understanding changing customer needs and providing them with high levels of satisfaction is an essential basis for building additional revenue and profit.

ACTION

▶ **Review your customers' purchasing patterns.**

▶ **Identify opportunities for additional sales.**

▶ **Assess the potential for building 'customers for life'.**

13

Controlling sales costs

Do you know the cost of winning new business?
How does it compare with the cost of retaining existing customers?
Is customer retention a worthwhile investment?

The cost of winning new business can be high – involving research, prospecting, progress meetings, proposals and development costs as well as the administrative costs of opening new accounts and setting up procedures to handle the work.

Customer loyalty programmes encourage customers to buy again, reducing sales development costs. For example, in a survey of car owners a high percentage said they would buy from the same dealer provided they enjoyed high levels of satisfaction. That requires an investment in customer care training and loyalty programmes, but the reward is in additional sales.

ACTION

▶ **Analyse your sales costs.**

▶ **Assess the cost of support programmes for retaining business.**

Contributing to long-term planning

Is your long-term planning based on an understanding of customers' real needs?

Would forecasts of repeat purchase add another dimension to the planning process?

Customer loyalty is an essential element in long-term planning. Understanding the customers' changing needs and being able to predict future purchases with a degree of accuracy contributes to the planning process. It helps to determine the direction of new product development and the introduction of services to support those customers.

ACTION

▶ **Build in forecasts of repeat purchase into your long-term planning process.**

Dealing with competitive activity

How could customer loyalty programmes help you deal with competitive activity?

Are your competitors using customer loyalty programmes?

Customer loyalty programmes build repeat business and help to deal with competitors. When customers enjoy high levels of satisfaction, they are not likely to be attracted by competitive activity. The best way to retain customers and deal with competitive activity is to provide the highest standards of customer service. However, programmes which make it simple for customers to buy from you can help to discourage competitive activity.

In business-to-business markets, companies use partnership and loyalty programmes to reduce levels of competition. By adding value to the relationship and helping customers develop their own business, a company can build close relationships with its customers and discourage them from going to other sources.

ACTION

► **Analyse competitive activity.**

► **Assess the impact of customer loyalty programmes on competitive activity.**

► **Develop programmes to deal with competitive activity.**

15

Summary

Building customer loyalty is not an isolated task; it is an integral part of managing every business. Operating customer loyalty programmes will have a significant impact on your long-term business prospects and will influence many of the other management actions that you and your team take. This chapter showed that you should review your business in the light of the following activities:

- improving long-term business performance;
- influencing product development;
- focusing the organisation on the customer;
- ensuring repeat purchase;
- increasing customer retention;
- shortening purchase cycles;
- enhancing the ownership experience;
- managing customer relationships;
- opening sales channels;

- controlling sales costs;
- contributing to long-term planning; and
- dealing with competitive activity.

By concentrating on improving performance in each of these areas, you will be able to:

- respond to customers' needs;
- differentiate your products or services from the competition; and
- build and retain long-term loyalty.

2

Allocating responsibility for customer loyalty

Customer loyalty is everyone's responsibility – or is it? In practice, it is often left to staff in sales, marketing or customer service – the people who are in regular contact with customers and who are in the best position to influence them. Customer loyalty is seen as a specific business programme or campaign, rather than an attitude which influences the whole organisation. The best books on customer care and customer service reinforce this message, but it's important to show how an attitude can be turned into practical actions. This chapter looks at the different departments in a typical company and explains how their attitudes and actions impact on customer loyalty. It also includes a series of management actions which can improve the contribution of each department.

Each of these departments has an impact on the customer, and their performance can make or break the reputation of the company:

- sales;
- distribution;
- manufacturing;
- purchasing;
- design and development;
- marketing;

- communications;
- personnel;
- training;
- customer service;
- administration;
- quality; and
- service.

Unfortunately, many of the people in these departments do not believe they are involved with customers – they deal with colleagues, supervisors or managers; they don't meet customers. But, by understanding how their actions can affect customer perceptions, each department can develop its own action programme to improve performance and help to build customer loyalty.

Sales

Sales staff doesn't just mean the people who meet customers face-to-face – the sales force – the people who handle sales administration – processing enquiries and progressing orders are just as important. Both groups play a frontline role in building customer loyalty – not just in dealing directly with customers, but ensuring that they get the right level of service from everyone in the organisation.

The sales force must develop a long-term focus but, to achieve this, there must be a shift in emphasis from selling to managing customer relationships – a task described as farming rather than hunting. Their main responsibility has been to maximise revenue; what they now have to do is spend more time with their customers developing relationships and possibly selling lower value products or services which help to maintain the contact between major sales. Building customer loyalty may not seem the number one priority for the sales force. This can lead to a conflict of interests, so it is important to structure the motivation and reward package so that it supports a loyalty programme.

The sales administration department is responsible for giving the sales force the right level of support; first, by providing a rapid and flexible response to customer enquiries because the right response will improve customer satisfaction. By processing orders promptly and ensuring that they are handled efficiently, the sales administration department will ensure that orders are delivered on time and that also helps to increase customer satisfaction. Just keeping customers up to date with progress on orders and deliveries can make a major contribution because people will accept change and delay provided they are kept informed.

Both the sales force and the sales administration staff have to work closely with other members of their own staff and with other members of the client team to build the right level of partnership. This in turn calls for new skills in developing relationships, managing and working with other people and managing time more effectively. Sales staff don't just need to develop their own skills, they have to build an effective support team to ensure that the customer gets the right level of service.

19

MANAGEMENT TASKS

- ▶ **Review sales force remuneration to ensure it encourages long-term relationships.**
- ▶ **Provide guidelines on the actions that will build customer loyalty.**
- ▶ **Develop sales force skills in managing relationships.**
- ▶ **Operate sales support programmes to build loyalty.**
- ▶ **Monitor the effectiveness of sales administration processes.**
- ▶ **Introduce quality standards for sales administration.**

Distribution

Nothing is more calculated to destroy the confidence of clients than poor delivery. Quality and added value are soon forgotten if the product fails to be there on the due date. But the people who are responsible for this are normally the ones who are least motivated to deliver customer care. They may have few responsibilities and be poorly paid, yet their role is crucial in:

- recognising the importance of internal as well as external customers;
- making sure the customer gets the right products – checking the delivery against the original order to see that everything is correct;
- maintaining close liaison with sales administration and manufacturing control so that they are aware of the urgency of deliveries;
- packing products properly so that they arrive in the best condition at the customer's premises and there is no loss of quality through damage;
- managing stock levels so that the company can provide a prompt efficient service; and
- knowing where to source alternatives when a product is out of stock.

Customers respond well – even when products are not immediately available – to the offer of getting them within a short timescale, but it is important to offer a realistic timescale. Customers will be delighted if the product is delivered before it was expected but they will be less happy if they come and it still hasn't arrived. They also expect distribution and warehouse staff to have a reasonable product knowledge so that they can deal quickly and effectively with requests for products. Training or efficient product information systems can help to improve the service customers get and ensure that they enjoy the right levels of convenience and satisfaction.

MANAGEMENT TASKS

- ▶ **Identify the distribution activities that influence customer loyalty.**
- ▶ **Introduce quality standards.**

▶ **Make distribution staff aware of their contribution.**

▶ **Look at communications between distributors and other departments such as manufacturing and sales.**

Manufacturing

Product quality is an integral part of customer satisfaction and loyalty and is the subject of many excellent books, so it will not be covered in detail here. But, customers don't just buy products – they buy a package of products, service, convenience and satisfaction. So in terms of customer loyalty, manufacturing management is responsible not just for the quality of the product, but for its efficient delivery, cost effectiveness and value for money.

It is vital to provide the right level of information to make sure that the customer is kept fully informed on the status of his orders. There may be ways of changing the manufacturing process or making modifications earlier in the design cycle.

21

MANAGEMENT TASKS

▶ **Work in close conjunction with colleagues in sales and the design/engineering departments to ensure total co-ordination of all the elements that are important in meeting the customers' requirements.**

▶ **Take the opportunity to participate in customer focus groups and in the evaluation of the results of customer satisfaction surveys.**

Manufacturing is not an isolated department that has no role to play in meeting customer requirements. It doesn't have a passive role in just producing products, it should be involved in pushing forward manufacturing standards and setting new quality standards. By insisting on the highest standards of quality control, better materials and engineering changes that will simplify or enhance the manufacturing process, or improve the performance and reliability of the product they can make their contribution to the enhancement of the product.

A vital part of the quality process is motivating staff to achieve the highest standards. Let your staff know when they have made significant improvements or achieved high levels of satisfaction – and let them know when things have gone wrong. They should be aware of customer concerns, the level of faults or returns. Use a black museum to show problems caused by poor manufacturing or quality control. People who are not aware of quality problems have no reason to change their standards.

Manufacturing is close to the vital edge and it must be able to make its full contribution to customer satisfaction.

Purchasing

Purchasing looks at first sight to be an unlikely candidate for building customer satisfaction and loyalty. The purchasing department needs to be aware of all the factors that affect customer satisfaction and loyalty so that they can incorporate these factors in their specifications. If, for example, research shows that companies need to make servicing simpler and more convenient so that owners still visit the dealer but pay less, the purchasing department has to source materials and components that will contribute to inherent reliability. If research shows that the company will have to extend its range then this means a new product range and sourcing opportunity.

By developing an effective working relationship with your main suppliers, your purchasing department can ensure that they meet the company's exacting standards. The purchasing department is ultimately responsible for the quality of the inputs to the manufacturing process and if they are not up to the required standard, then the quality of the product will ultimately suffer. They also need to ensure prompt effective delivery so that the customer gets the product when he needs it.

Many purchasing departments are going much further and building strategic alliances with their suppliers. By reducing the number of suppliers and working with a selected few who meet the standards, they are able to achieve much higher standards; for example, by insisting that their suppliers integrate their quality systems with the company so that quality is assured at every stage. By insisting on a standard quality registration, they can ensure product consistency and that is central to customer loyalty. They can also ask suppliers to integrate their information systems so that they can always have access to status information and keep all departments informed of the situation.

By working closely with other departments, such as manufacturing, design and sales administration, purchasing can influence the direction of customer satisfaction.

Design and development

23

Product design has a direct effect on customer loyalty. By designing products and services that meet customers' changing needs the design department can help to encourage repurchase and build loyalty. New product development programmes need to be tightly focused on customer requirements and research so that the company is customer-driven rather than product-driven.

- Are you aware of product and customer research?
- Keep up to date with competitive developments through trade press and visits to exhibitions.
- Rank your development programme against factors that customers see as important.
- Put the emphasis on improving the performance, reliability, convenience and serviceability of products and services.

The design department can get even more involved by taking part in customer focus groups, industry associations and customer liaison panels. This provides a two-way benefit – designers get to understand customers' real needs and hear their problems at first hand, and they are able to keep them up to date with technical developments. Some companies consult their customers at different stages of the development process to keep them up to date with technical developments and to allow them to comment on the direction of the design process. This means that customers are involved in the new product development process and feel that they are working in partnership with the supplier.

This process can be made even more formal by handling contract research and development or by taking on customisation programmes for individual customers. Here the supplier acts as an integral part of the customer's operations and is clearly involved with the future development of the business.

It is vital that design and development work closely with purchasing, manufacturing and marketing to ensure that their work is integrated.

MANAGEMENT TASKS

► **Is marketing aware of the latest design specifications?**
► **Do they understand the significance of new product developments in terms of the marketing edge?**
► **Can manufacturing utilise design changes to improve product performance and reliability?**
► **Is purchasing aware of the design and performance requirements of the components they buy in?**

Marketing

Marketing has traditionally been the department that is closest to the customer. Companies have moved from being production-led to being marketing-led, but that focus is now becoming even tighter and marketing has become just one element of the drive to build customer loyalty. Marketing staff provide the vital link between the customer and the organisation. Because they play such a pivotal role they are in an ideal position to drive a customer loyalty programme forward, develop products and services to support it, introduce loyalty programmes, influence the direction of communications and monitor the feedback from the programme.

Customer care programmes are often originated in the marketing department to ensure that everything reflects what the customer really needs.

Marketing is also concerned with the way the products are presented to the marketplace in terms of their packaging and distribution. Are the products designed to be easily accessible and do they convey to the customer that the company really cares for their interests?

Marketing works closely with most departments so it can have a useful co-ordinating role and it will be sure to have its eyes firmly on the customer at all times.

MANAGEMENT TASKS

► **Is the company marketing programme focused on customer satisfaction and loyalty?**

► **Does the department have budget and resources to support customer loyalty programmes?**

► **Do all marketing activities include elements of customer loyalty?**

Communications

Communication plays a vital role in every aspect of customer loyalty and it is also the essential link between the various departments of the company who are responsible for building customer satisfaction. There may not be a separate communications department – it may be a function of marketing – but it is essential that the activity is carefully managed to get the greatest possible benefit.

The process starts inside the organisation; list every department involved in building customer loyalty – sales, distribution, retail, manufacturing, design/development, marketing, quality, personnel, training, purchasing, customer service, and administration.

The communications plan should identify the key people in each of those groups – the managers and supervisors and the staff who are dealing directly with customers. It is vital that they are fully briefed on their responsibilities and that they are kept continually up to date with the company's progress and new product developments as well as the customer loyalty programmes.

A communications manual can provide reference for the people who have to implement the programme and give them a useful place to keep copies of all relevant information. External communications too are vital to the success of the programme, so the department has to establish a contact strategy and see that it is implemented. The strategy will include a description of the target audience and their concerns, together with the key messages which will position the company as a caring organisation that wants to continue doing business with those customers. If a company wants to build partnership with key accounts, the communications department will need to work closely with the account management team to ensure that the right communications are being individually targeted at the right accounts.

Communications are an integral part of the whole customer loyalty process – they are not a separate activity and although they are likely to be carried out by a separate department they should be integrated into every type of activity.

MANAGEMENT TASKS

- ► **Are key staff aware of their responsibility?**
- ► **Do they understand the communication programmes and strategies for building loyalty?**
- ► **Are your internal communications consistently building an image of a caring organisation?**
- ► **Are individuals and departments who communicate with customers following corporate guidelines?**

Personnel

Focusing on customer loyalty can mean a considerable culture change in an organisation and the personnel department will be directly involved. For example, staff will have to be redeployed and trained for key customer support tasks and new staff may have to be recruited to fill gaps. Recruitment advertising is the starting point – it should highlight the fact that the company is driven by customers and to achieve that it needs to recruit people of the highest calibre who are committed to customer care. Recruitment advertisements convey to customers that the company has a positive attitude to its people. By stressing the training and caring opportunities and the ways in which service can be improved by better people, the company shows that it is committed to customer service.

For its part, the company will operate a policy of people care which will ensure that everyone gets the chance to develop their own personal and business skills and that their contribution to the company's achievements will be recognised. The company's induction process and employee information programme should help people to understand their role and contribution and to know what is expected of them. The personnel department needs to:

- lay down customer focus standards;
- give clear specific instructions on how to achieve the standards;
- outline the personal and business skills needed to achieve those objectives; and
- describe the training that is available to build the skills.

Direct involvement by the personnel department helps to instill the right attitudes in personnel and helps to ensure that the company has a committed workforce that will enable the company to meet its business objectives.

As a result, the company will be able to deliver quality solutions through quality people and this will ensure that all the resources are in position to meet the company's business objectives.

MANAGEMENT TASKS

▶ **Develop a skills profile to support a customer-focused organisation.**

▶ **Integrate customer satisfaction messages into all recruitment, training and employee communications.**

▶ **Operate a people-care programme.**

▶ **Define the requirements of customer loyalty programmes.**

Training

Closely allied to the personnel function is training. Customer loyalty needs high standards of personal and business skills development so the training department has to work closely with all the departments who are responsible for customer satisfaction and loyalty programmes to identify the skills needed. The programme should start with the people who are directly involved in the front line but eventually it will include everyone in the organisation whose actions impact on customer loyalty. When all the key people have been trained in customer-care skills, the result is a customer-facing organisation.

Implementing this kind of far-reaching training programme takes considerable resources, so it needs to be sold at different levels:

- senior management – to get their commitment and buy in to the resources and funds needed to get the training programme under way;

- departmental managers – whose staff will be involved in delivering the customer loyalty programmes; they need to know how the training will improve the performance of the department and how it will help them to deliver the right sort of service; they also need to know what sort of commitment in terms of time and numbers of people will be involved;

- staff – they need to know how they will benefit from the training and what it involves; and

- training staff including managers and senior executives – briefing them will help to ensure they know how to get the best out of their staff.

The training programmes will cover both programme and personal skills – the programme skills will include an introduction to any customer loyalty programmes that are operating together with detailed guidance on how to use them. The personal skills are wide-ranging, covering aspects of personal care, understanding customer requirements and delivering the highest levels of customer satisfaction.

MANAGEMENT TASKS

▶ **Develop a skills profile of a customer-facing organisation.**

▶ **Get the commitment of executives, departmental managers, staff and training specialists.**

▶ **Make sure training covers personal and programme skills.**

Customer service

A company may not have a customer service department – in fact some writers have suggested that it should be banned. Customer service departments were set up originally to handle complaints or deal with queries. They were a gesture to customer care, and they did have the advantage of being highly visible. The problem is that it suggests customer care is limited to one department in the company and that conflicts with the view that everyone is involved in building customer loyalty. However, it provides a focal point for the customer when it is used as a 'front desk' for the company, allowing a single access point for all services and enquiries. So if a customer has a query, but doesn't know whom to contact he can be put in touch with the right person by someone who knows. This is in sharp contrast to the experience of being passed from one extension to another or being left on the end of a line that nobody answers.

To do this 'front desk' job properly the contact needs to be familiar with all the departments in the company and needs to have good customer handling techniques. Here are some ways of making the most of a customer service desk.

- Log the queries that come in through this route because it can provide useful clues to the sort of queries customers have.

- Equip the contact staff with information on customers so that they can provide an informed response. For example, computerised records giving customer details, purchases, service history and past queries.

- Record and analyse customer complaints – this can help to guide the future development of the products and services.

- Provide staff with the right level of authority to be able to deal with complaints without having to keep referring back to a higher authority.

- Introduce an escalation process so that if a problem cannot be resolved satisfactorily, then after a set period of time the issue will automatically be escalated up to a higher level in the company.

The customer service department should not be seen as a wall which prevents customer complaints getting into the organisation.

MANAGEMENT TASKS

- ▶ **Review the role of customer service.**
- ▶ **Ensure that the organisation has a clearly defined, well equipped front desk.**
- ▶ **Monitor and analyse the queries that come through the front desk.**
- ▶ **Develop a caring, positive attitude to customer complaints.**

Administration

Administration can be one of the weak links in a company's

customer satisfaction performance, because it is the little things that can upset customers. For example, orders which are telephoned through and then not processed correctly can lead to incorrect delivery and a broken schedule which affects the customer's own business. Recurring faults like that are not the best way to retain customer loyalty. Invoicing is frequently cited as one of the most difficult areas for companies to get right. Customers receive bills for products or services they have not bought, the amounts are incorrect or they do not quote purchasing reference numbers, which causes the customer system to reject them.

It is worth examining administrative procedures in more detail because this is where a reputation for quality can stand or fall.

- Always quote the customer order number so that the customer can relate to the documentation in his own system.
- Final figures should bear some relation to the numbers that were quoted originally.
- Explain any changes. This helps the customer to deal with the invoices within his own system.
- Information should be clearly presented and should be as informative as possible.

Administration is seen as a Cinderella activity, but it is an essential part of aftercare.

MANAGEMENT TASKS

- ► Look at opportunities to improve administrative procedures.
- ► Incorporate comments on administration in satisfaction surveys and analyse the response.
- ► Make staff aware of customer response implications of administration.
- ► Look for opportunities to integrate company and customer reporting and administrative systems.

31

Quality

Quality is a prerequisite for customer loyalty, but it is not a self-contained activity. Quality should be integral to every company activity. It is the responsibility of a quality manager to identify where the priorities should be and to implement the processes. In an organisation that is driven by the customer, quality should be applied to every customer-facing activity. Manufacturing is normally the key area for quality control and this is dealt with in detail in other books. But it actually begins further back than that with the process of customer reception. The processes by which customer enquiries are handled can be measured and quality controlled. For example, how long does it take for the phone to be answered and if the call is a query how long does it take for the caller to get a response?

By analysing and improving the process, customers will get the right impression of the organisation immediately. The delivery of services can also be measured and quantified so that people know how long they should expect to wait to get certain tasks completed. A good example of this is the way the public utilities have set high standards for responding to service calls from the public and if they fail to meet them they agree to pay certain levels of compensation. This is quality assurance at its best and it shows that it goes beyond the manufacturing process.

Quality can also be applied to areas like information, instructions, the accuracy of invoicing and the way in which companies respond to requests for quotations. The company has to look at all aspects of its operations to see whether there are any critical processes which should be included in the quality process.

MANAGEMENT TASKS

► **Where should quality be applied in your organisation?**

► **Can you apply quality standards to these processes?**

► **How many of the processes affect customer loyalty?**

Service department

The service department can be the company's strongest link with the customer. By developing a wide-ranging service strategy, they can maintain a high level of contact with the customer, but it's essential that these contacts are of the highest quality. First of all service staff must have the technical skills and the support infrastructure to deliver the highest levels of service. This means investing in service technology and support and developing the skills to use it to full effect.

It is also important that there is the right sort of response to a service request. Customers expect engineers to be well prepared for handling a problem before they arrive. That way, they feel confident that the engineer will arrive with the right parts and the skills to carry out the repair. This calls for good diagnostic skills and the ability to use database information as a basis for planning and forecasting repairs. If the fault can't be identified in advance, the engineer must have the confidence to know when and where he can get information to help. Above all, customers want confidence. If the problem can't be fixed right away, they want to be given clear accurate advice on when it will happen.

The service engineer is an ideal person to influence the perceptions of the customer – customers tend to trust engineers rather than salespeople and engineers can often be asked for their advice on selecting future equipment. They in turn can provide advice and information on what customers need and they can be a valuable source of market information. Companies are now building care visits into their service contact strategy.

Good service can be the driving force that differentiates one product from another in a crowded marketplace.

MANAGEMENT TASKS

► **Make sure customers have an opportunity to comment on service through visit cards and satisfaction surveys.**

33

▶ **Take advantage of an engineer's presence on site to get customer information and build trusting relationships.**

▶ **Use customer service to build long-term relationships.**

Summary

Building customer loyalty is everyone's responsibility. However, many departments within a company do not have direct contact with customers and feel that they cannot contribute to customer loyalty. This chapter looked at the potential contribution of each of the following departments:

- sales;
- distribution;
- manufacturing;
- purchasing;
- design and development;
- marketing;
- communications;
- personnel;
- training;
- customer service;
- administration;
- quality; and
- service.

Key management tasks are identified for each department and these ensure that staff:

- understand their role in building customer loyalty;
- review their activities against customer focus standards; and
- put action programmes into operation.

3

Identifying opportunities

Building customer loyalty is not an extra activity – it is an integral part of every management task. However, the search for opportunities to build customer loyalty is a continuous task and one that should be pursued with real effort. This chapter describes a number of techniques for identifying opportunities.

Aftercare

Every contact with the customer helps to build loyalty.

Parts and service operations can generate 500 per cent more contacts than initial sales contacts.

Have you got a planned aftercare programme?

The aftermarket provides the greatest opportunity for building customer loyalty through regular quality contact. One automotive manufacturer reckoned to make five million contacts a year through parts and service operations compared with one million contacts for new car sales.

- Do your products need regular servicing, repair or spare parts?
- Are your customers likely to need access to an enquiry or technical service?
- Do you provide your customers with a customer service or complaints department?

It is not sufficient just to provide aftercare. Unless the service operates to a high standard, it will not build customer satisfaction and loyalty. Quality aftercare helps to differentiate products.

- Have you got the resources to set up your own aftercare operation?
- Can you control the standards of aftercare provided by third parties to your customers?

The models later in the book provide examples of aftercare programmes for a wide range of businesses.

Customer services

Companies spend large sums of money on training, maintenance and other services to support products.

These services are often provided by company staff or other suppliers.

Manufacturers are missing out on a major customer loyalty opportunity if they do not provide customer services.

Few companies have exploited the power of services to build business and customer loyalty. Recently, a major engineering group announced that it intended to become a global services company. The market was changing and its major customers in government and industry were spending increasing amounts of their budget on maintaining and managing the equipment they had bought. But, given the cost constraints on their customers, the group recognised that much of the work could be handled more efficiently by outside suppliers.

- What kind of services are your customers likely to need?
- How do your customers provide or source these services?
- Do they have the skills to provide their own services?
- Could you carry out the same services more cost effectively or to a higher standard?
- Are competitors or other organisations providing the services efficiently or cost effectively?

■ Can you work with other organisations to provide the full range of services your customers need?

■ Have you used life cycle analysis (described later in this chapter) to identify the types of service needed?

Information systems companies have made good use of services to maintain regular contact with their customers. They have developed new skills and techniques to carry out increasingly sophisticated levels of maintenance which are beyond the reach of customer staff or independent maintenance organisations. In many cases, they don't provide all the services themselves, but manage other external resources or work with chosen business partners and control the quality of their service. This can ensure that the customer gets the right level of service, but without the investment in a service infrastructure.

37

Total business solutions

To make the best use of your product, your customer may need training, advice, support and many other services.

Obtaining services from different sources is time-consuming.

Offering customers a total business solution builds greater loyalty than just delivering a product.

A total business solution is also known as a turnkey solution – all the customer has to do is switch on the equipment and it's particularly appropriate in sectors like information systems. The manufacturer, instead of just supplying the equipment and leaving installation and management to the customer, now provides all the services needed to ensure successful use of the equipment.

The customer gets a better return on his investment while the supplier earns additional revenue from services and gets the opportunity to maintain contact.

■ Do you understand your customers' business objectives, their resources and the costs of their operations?

- Have you analysed all the factors your customers need to consider to succeed with your product?

- Can you provide or manage all the services your customer needs?

- Can you deliver those services in a package that simplifies your customers' administration?

- Does your customer need to make changes in his own organisation to benefit from your product and can you help him achieve those changes?

Providing your customer with a total solution doesn't just build customer loyalty, it can make you a dependent supplier and provide you with additional revenue from services and management contracts.

The models in Part II provide examples of total business solutions.

Complaints analysis

Complaints handled correctly can improve levels of customer satisfaction.

Complaints provide an opportunity to improve your products and your standards of customer service.

Is a customer complaint an indication of failure or an opportunity to respond and show that the company is concerned? Research shows that customers who have their complaints resolved are likely to repurchase, while those who still feel dissatisfied will go elsewhere. There are two types of complaint – one where isolated customers receive a faulty product or poor service and one where there is a recurring problem. In both cases, the complaint should be a starting point for action.

- Have you got a procedure in place for handling, recording and monitoring complaints?

- Have you set up a corrective action programme to ensure that customer concerns are managed properly?

- Do you respond promptly to customer complaints?

- Have you got a structured response mechanism so that people get a response at the right level? If, for example, a sales manager should not be able to resolve the issue, the problem immediately passes right up to director level until it is resolved.

Take a positive look at the complaints you receive from your customers because they give you the opportunity to respond. By encouraging complaints, you keep your customers talking – it's difficult to respond to customers who have complained with their feet.

Customer research

Customer research keeps you in contact with customers.
Research involves customers in your business.

To build customer loyalty, you must continue to meet your customers' changing needs. Research tells you what your customers are looking for and you can use research information to shape your own future product development.

- What kind of research does your company carry out?
- Is the information suitable for identifying customer loyalty requirements?
- Analyse customer research carefully to identify factors that customers prefer in competitive products or your own.
- Are you stressing the benefits that research shows are most important to customers?
- What do your customers like about your products and those of your competitors?

Customer focus panels are another form of market research in which groups of customers meet with company staff to give their opinions on different aspects of the company's products and services. They can be used on an ad-hoc basis or as a means of monitoring progress over a period of time.

Focus panels have two customer loyalty benefits – they help to identify what customers want and they also maintain contact.

By asking customers' opinions and involving them in decisions about products and services, the company is showing that it cares about their attitudes. Customer focus panels also help people inside the company gain a better understanding of customers' needs and this can help to create a customer-driven culture.

To make the most of customer focus panels it is important that the right people from the company are involved and that they are in a position to respond to the suggestions and take actions.

- What opportunities are there for using customer focus panels?
- Who are the key customers who should be involved?
- Are there industry liaison groups who could provide the right level of customer focus?
- Who should be involved from your organisation?
- How do you plan to respond to the panel's suggestion or criticism?

Customer surveys

Surveys tell customers you welcome their views.

Survey results can focus attention on the need for improvements.

Responding to survey results demonstrates the highest levels of customer care.

This is another form of market research which can help companies focus on the needs of their customers. The surveys take a number of forms:

- regular surveys on product performance or service delivery – the results are used to build up a picture of cumulative trends; and
- surveys of customer satisfaction with a range of products or services over a period of time – the ratings for different products

or for different branch performance are compared to provide a complete picture of customer satisfaction levels.

- Do you survey your customers' attitudes to the products and services you provide?
- Do you analyse results and take corrective action where appropriate?
- Do you let customers know what actions you are taking to improve performance?
- Are you making customers aware of their contribution to your business success?

Competitive activity

Are you aware of what your competitors are doing to build customer satisfaction?

How does your performance compare with your competitors?

What standards should you be aiming at to achieve the highest levels of customer loyalty?

Another way of identifying customer loyalty opportunities is to monitor competitive activity. How should the company position itself against competition? Should it aim to set industry best standards or should it simply match the competition?

A benchmark is a means of identifying industry best practice for a product or service. By aiming at best in industry standards a company can convince customers and staff that it is committed to quality standards.

- Look at the results of market research on attitudes to competitive products.
- Find out what customers like about competitive products or services and find out how your own product or service compares.
- Check the media to see what kind of loyalty programmes your customers are running. That way you can either match or improve them.

■ Use mystery shopper techniques to find out how competitors are trying to retain customers and make sure you can counter their moves.

Monitoring competitive activity is an integral part of planning your customer loyalty programmes, but the risk is that your programmes may be purely reactive and not represent the best that your company can offer.

Adding value

Differentiate your products from your competitors by adding value.
Plan the added value elements to encourage customer loyalty.

42

Adding value to a product or service can help to differentiate products from the competition and to build customer loyalty. Analyse each of the products and services in your range to see how you can add value and improve the customers' perception of the product.

■ Business services that free customer staff to do more important tasks or help a manager perform his or her job better add value to the basic product.

■ Training, for example, can help a company to make more of the products that they buy by ensuring that staff can make the most effective use of them.

■ Accessories can make a consumer product such as a camera more attractive.

■ Sometimes the techniques and examples of added value are more subtle. Management consultancies, for example, who offer their customers invitations to seminars or who offer them business books are helping customers to improve their own performance.

Added value can be a powerful weapon in building customer loyalty because it helps to show that the customer can benefit from more than the product.

Life cycle analysis

Customers' needs change during the life cycle of a product.

By recognising these changing needs and providing relevant products or services, you can build customer loyalty.

Every product goes through a life cycle and this can give important clues to the additional products and services a customer might need. Customers' needs change as they progress through the life cycle. They may need help in introducing a product, making the best use of it or preparing for change.

The stages are called:

- pre-sales consultancy;
- getting started;
- keeping going; and
- going further.

To identify the life cycle for your products:

- review the way your customers use your products;
- can it be easily divided into life cycle stages?
- analyse recent sales records to determine which stage of the life cycle your customers are in.

Before a customer buys a product, he may need advice and guidance on the type of product that is most suitable for his needs. The opportunity here is to provide pre-sales consultancy or planning. This can take a number of forms – strategic consultancy, technical consultancy, feasibility studies or other planning services. Although the service may be seen as a free 'cost of sale' service, the fact that it helps the customer formulate his plans makes it a valuable service and one that can be charged. This type of service can also help the company secure business against competition by maintaining the right level of contact at a strategic level.

- How do your customers buy your products or services?

43

- Can you help them by providing planning or consultancy services?
- Do you have the skills and resources to offer planning services?
- Are you increasing revenue by charging for these services?
- Are you taking every opportunity to contact customers before a major purchase?

After a customer has bought a product, he may need help in 'getting started'. The customer is unfamiliar with the product and may need help in making use of it. The services could include installation, initial training for users, project management to provide additional start-up services not available to the customer.

- How complex is the product – do customers need training?
- Is the product difficult to install?
- Will the customers need help to introduce the product?

The main stage in the product life cycle is 'keeping going' where the product is in regular use and is paying for itself. The important service here is routine maintenance to ensure that the product keeps performing to its designed level.

- Are you handling the maintenance of the product?
- Do your customers need help in managing the product?
- Have you got a stand-by service to help customers in trouble?

The final stage is 'taking it further' – the customers may be redefining their business requirements or there may be a change in the business environment. The services at this stage could include optimisation studies, upgrades, performance monitoring or consultancy.

- Are you aware of any changes in your customers' business conditions?
- Could you recommend ways in which your customers could make better use of your product?

The life cycle is an ideal way to identify opportunities. The important thing is that, as companies identify each stage, they should be developing plans to provide products and services for the next stage. By anticipating the customers' needs and helping them prepare for a successful transition, the company can build partnership.

Summary

Every business must take positive action to build customer loyalty. Before that process begins, it is important to be aware of the actions that can have the greatest impact on customer loyalty. This chapter described how to identify opportunities in your company by:

- developing a planned aftercare programme to maintain contact after the sale;
- providing services which your customers need to make effective use of your products;
- offering a total business solution so that your customers depend on you as a single source of supply;
- analysing complaints and taking corrective action so that you can overcome problems, rather than lose customers;
- carrying out research into customers' needs;
- operating customer surveys so that customers have a clearly defined route for consultation;
- monitoring competitive activity to see where you can make further improvements;
- adding value to your products so that you differentiate your products from the competition; and
- analysing your customers' business life cycles so that you can identify opportunities to provide relevant products or services.

This chapter has provided a framework for identifying opportunities and has shown that companies must develop plans and products to take advantage of those opportunities.

4

Taking the initiative

Making customer loyalty a priority

Companies depend on customers for their survival and pro-fitability. The customer must be the number one focus and all corporate policies must be driven by customer needs. But how does customer loyalty become a priority?

- Start by making it a high profile activity.
- Make sure everyone in the organisation is aware of customer loyalty.
- Get your staff together and explain that building customer loyalty is everyone's responsibility; it's not something that can be passed on to other people and other departments.
- Drive home the message that every action the company takes influences customer loyalty, whether it's answering the telephone, designing products, sending out an invoice or delivering the goods.
- Provide your staff with the information and skills they need to provide the highest standards of customer care.

Getting top-level commitment

The process of building customer loyalty begins at the top. Unless senior managers are seen to be committed, there is a risk that the task will not be seen as important. Getting top-level commitment means allocating resources, funds and people to push through critical tasks. Senior managers need to set the standards for customer satisfaction – to say where the company is going and what it will ultimately achieve. They set the overall quality goals.

Senior managers also need to get close to customers by:

- getting involved in regular meetings;
- making special trips to customer premises;
- handling complaints at senior level; and
- talking to the people who are delivering customer service.

Setting standards

A customer loyalty programme must have standards so that staff know what is expected of them. For example, if the strategy is to build customer loyalty by making it easier for customers to order products or get information, set target response times or dispatch times and measure performance against the standard. 'We aim to respond to all sales enquiries within four hours' or 'our target is to dispatch all orders within twenty-four hours'.

- Identify the business activities that will help you build customer loyalty.
- Set targets for each and explain how performance will be measured.
- Implement any actions that need to be taken to ensure that the targets can be achieved and maintained.
- Publish the targets throughout the organisation and make people fully aware of their own responsibilities and standards.
- Publish the targets for your customers and let them know how you are progressing against those targets.

Ranking customer requirements

By analysing the results of surveys and other market research, you will gain a better understanding of your customers' needs and you can base your future product development plans on those needs. However, customer requirements may not always be realistic and sometimes the changes they suggest may not yield real customer loyalty benefits. So customer requirements have to be ranked to ensure that the company is focusing on the right priorities.

- Set out customers' key requirements.
- Lay down a route for meeting those requirements.
- Establish who should be responsible for meeting those requirements.
- Determine what actions should be taken to improve performance through service development or personal skills training.

Customer requirements will help the organisation to set realistic achievable targets such as 'we aim to offer the best possible delivery in the business', or 'we want to offer the highest quality of legal advice' or 'we want to make sure that our business is known for delivering the highest standards of maintenance'. By focusing on specific actions, staff can commit themselves to achieving measurable results rather than just talking about loyalty.

Setting key performance objectives

To achieve the customer standards, set departmental objectives for all the areas of improvement. Key performance objectives allow the company to integrate its business objectives with its customer care objectives. An example of the customer care objectives might be 'we want to offer the best and fastest pizza delivery'. The business objective would be to set up a delivery infrastructure which would support that and to train the delivery staff to achieve the highest levels of customer care.

Identifying opportunities for improvement

The drive for customer loyalty forces companies to look closely at the way they deliver their product or service and to see how it can be improved. By setting specific standards and objectives, the company has a clear route ahead and it knows where investment is likely to produce the greatest rewards. Customer research, feedback on performance and analysis of complaints will help to determine where the main effort should go.

- Set up a procedure for monitoring the company's performance in critical areas and implement an on-going programme of improvement where this will provide additional business benefit.
- Make sure that these improvements get the resources they need to drive them through.
- Ensure that they are completed within a timescale.
- Let customers and employees know about the improvements – it's another good opportunity to contact people and to demonstrate that the company cares.

49

Issuing a statement of direction

Customers and staff want to know where the company is going and this can be achieved through a statement of direction or mission statement, as it's sometimes known. This provides a framework for integrating a whole range of customer loyalty activities.

A statement of direction should be clear and should be achievable; an unrealistic aim such as becoming the most profitable company in the world will not be believable and this can lower staff commitment. Far better to be specific: 'to be seen as providing a caring service'.

Statements of direction are important for customers because they can be reassured that futur developments will be in line with their own business objectives. This can help them plan their own future product development and will make it easier to work in partnership. They can also see that the company is committed to

c

their business and this will help them to build the right sort of relationship.

Allocating responsibilities

Customer loyalty programmes need to be driven by people who have both commitment and responsibility – people sometimes referred to as 'champions' because they are capable of pushing through change against all the odds. Although everyone in the organisation should be committed to customer loyalty, there are certain groups of staff who play a key role in building loyalty and it's important that they have a clear understanding of their responsibilities. Get together a project team of people from all the important departments and make sure they have the authority and the resources to carry out their actions.

Summary

Customer loyalty programmes must be driven. Without a strong sense of direction and urgency, they will drift and staff will lose interest after an initial burst of enthusiasm. This chapter explained how managers can introduce customer loyalty programmes and maintain the momentum by:

- making customer loyalty a priority so that everyone in the organisation is aware of its importance;
- getting top-level commitment to ensure that the programmes have adequate funding and resources;
- setting standards so that staff understand what they have to achieve to build customer loyalty;
- ranking customer requirements to ensure that the company's resources are concentrated on the most productive tasks;
- setting key performance objectives as a basis for training and funding;

- identifying opportunities for improvement and responding to research and customer feedback;

- issuing a statement of direction to ensure that future developments are in line with the customer loyalty strategy; and

- allocating responsibility for managing the programme and individual activities.

All of these activities underpin the specific customer loyalty programmes and ensure that the programme moves forward in a planned, integrated way.

51

5

Building staff commitment and understanding

Creating a customer-focused environment

The commitment and involvement of staff is essential to customer loyalty. You need to involve people at all levels in the recommendations, decisions and actions you take to build customer loyalty. That way, you maximise the use of your people's talents and at the same time achieve their active commitment. The power of people to improve performance is enormous when they are committed.

To achieve this, you need to take a number of actions:

- provide information at all levels, including information which in the past might have been regarded as confidential and open only to top management;

- improve co-operation across all departmental functions so that people understand and are committed to your business objectives.;

- improve the quality and attitude of your people by actively encouraging staff to develop their own skills through training and career development; and

- encourage people who have taken their own customer care initiatives.

Customer loyalty is built on quality service and the key to that is the quality of people.

- Recruit people who are motivated to succeed through achievement.
- Provide staff with continuous specialist and quality training to develop their own personal skills.
- Ensure that staff understand the customers' requirements for the highest standards of service.

Auditing staff understanding

If a customer loyalty initiative is to succeed, it must have the commitment of everyone in the organisation who has a direct or indirect effect on customer perceptions and attitudes. Traditionally only front-line staff, such as sales people or service engineers were seen to have an influence on customers. The reality is that everyone in the company affects customer perceptions in some way. Storemen who supply the wrong part or technicians who leave a customer's car in a dirty condition create negative perceptions.

The internal communications supporting a customer loyalty programme should explain the role of individuals in the overall strategy and give them a sense of pride in their contribution. It should also seek to build team spirit and eliminate any weak links in the process of maximising customer satisfaction.

Before the process of building commitment begins, it is important to identify the current level of awareness of customer loyalty issues through a communications audit. This is an example of a communications audit used to assess a marketing communications plan and form the basis for planning specific marketing communications initiatives.

The audit concentrates on three key questions:

1 What is the level of awareness of customer loyalty issues within the company?

2 How consistently are customer loyalty messages presented?

3 How effectively do customer loyalty communications support the sales process?

INTERNAL AWARENESS OF CUSTOMER LOYALTY ISSUES

Customer loyalty communications cut across traditional company boundaries, impacting on perceptions of the company as a whole and on perceptions of individual departments. It is therefore important that customer loyalty messages are understood and presented consistently throughout the company. Research should be carried out within the company to assess the understanding of customer loyalty issues at corporate level, and within product groups and departments responsible for customer contact.

Objectives

- Identify key internal audiences for customer loyalty communications.
- Assess level and effectiveness of internal customer loyalty communications.

Technique

Interviews with selected people from:

- marketing and communications staff;
- departmental managers;
- the sales force; and
- corporate PR and communications staff.

CONSISTENT PRESENTATION OF CUSTOMER LOYALTY MESSAGES

The audit would look at the content of communications projects to ensure that it reflected current customer loyalty positioning messages and was relevant to the information needs of the target audience. Presentations, brochures, videos, internal communications, advertisements and press information should incorporate consistent customer loyalty messages.

Objectives

- Measure how consistently customer loyalty messages are communicated.
- Identify mechanisms for controlling communications consistency.

Scope

- Marketing publications.
- Sales proposals.
- Corporate communications.

Technique

- Review published material.
- Interview communications managers/authors.

EFFECTIVE SUPPORT OF THE SALES PROCESS

Considerable opportunities exist for developing customer loyalty through the salesforce. The audit should assess the level of customer loyalty awareness within the sales force and look at the potential for increasing motivation to build loyalty.

The sales force currently receive information on products and marketing developments from all product groups. The audit will consider whether the customer loyalty information they receive is relevant to their information needs, and whether it is presented in a convenient, persuasive form.

The audit will consider all the channels of sales force communication available to assess which would be the most effective for customer loyalty messages.

Objectives

- Measure the contribution of customer loyalty programmes to the sales process.

Scope

- Awareness of customer loyalty issues.

- Awareness of customer loyalty support material.
- Use and value of support material.
- Perceived sales support requirements.

Technique

- Interviews with sales force and sales managers.
- Audit of use of customer loyalty programmes.
- Develop model of sales process/deliverables.

Demonstrating individual contribution

It is sometimes difficult to convince individuals that their contribution matters. In some cases the contribution is obvious – customer care manager, receptionist, quality manager – but when someone is carrying out a specialist function, how can you convince them that their actions influence customer loyalty?

Here is an extract from a staff handbook on customer care.

> 'This booklet is not about the technical details of your job . . . it is about your contribution to customer satisfaction. . . . Successful performance depends on a high standard of customer care and attention.'

Sales and reception staff are in regular contact with customers. By giving help and attention to their customers, they create trust and respect – and they are building customer loyalty. A technician's job is not like that – they rarely see customers, let alone talk to them. But if a technician does his job properly, the customers' product performs well. Because the customer is satisfied, he or she comes back next time they want work done.

The handbook then describes a series of actions the technician can take to build customer satisfaction. It is important that these actions are not abstract, but reflect the technician's job directly.

'Take pride in your work . . . look after the customer's property . . . don't take short cuts . . . don't take things for granted . . . do a thorough job.'

Each of those messages is backed by a series of specific lists related to the actual job. The most effective of these messages is 'take pride in your work' because that appeals directly to the technician's professionalism.

'Guessing the cause of a fault without a proper check is the hallmark of a poor technician. Rely on your skills . . . use every chance to go on adding to your skills and knowledge . . . set yourself high personal quality standards.'

This approach ensures that the technician understands the direct relationship between his personal skills and customer satisfaction.

57

Use this approach to demonstrate the contribution that key members of staff can make. Analyse their job description to see where their actions impact on customers. Draw up an action plan for each individual.

Identifying customer expectations

For many members of staff, the opportunities to meet customers are rare. Technicians rarely see customers face to face. When they do, it's usually to sort out a serious problem, so it's difficult to build commitment to the customer. However, by making staff aware of what the customer wants and, more importantly, doesn't want, that helps to build understanding.

Here is another example from the handbook.

'When a customer comes to the service department, he wants prompt and helpful attention. He doesn't want any nasty surprises like a much higher bill than he expected. And he wants the product to keep on working efficiently until it's time for the next service.'

It is also important to realise what the customer doesn't want.

- A job not done, either the main job not completed or another job overlooked.

- Reporting that no fault can be found when a problem exists – ask the technician how he would feel if he were the customer.

- Worse still, if the customer finds fault with the equipment when he gets it home or if the fault recurs after a couple of days, levels of customer satisfaction drop dramatically.

These are the serious problems that technicians should be aware of. However, it's often the little things that get overlooked which can cause the most irritation.

In the car repair business, for example, small things such as cigarette ends in the ashtray of a non-smoker, the radio tuned to a different station, grease marks on the steering wheel or car body can all cause irritation.

By reporting customer concerns directly, in terms the technician can understand, the message comes across more strongly.

Targeting key staff

While it is essential to let all your staff know how they can contribute to customer loyalty, it is equally important to get the highest standards of performance from key staff whose actions have a direct impact on the customer – the customer-facing staff who are in regular contact and who are seen by the customers as the personification of the company. By identifying those people and analysing the skills they need to achieve the highest levels of satisfaction, the company can concentrate its training and resources on key activities.

Sales staff for example have to undergo major changes in attitude if they are to adopt a customer care role. Sales force performance is vital to effective management of customer relationships, but sometimes sales staff are more concerned with the drive for short-term maximisation of revenue and this can interfere with building long-term relationships. Continuity of contact, for example, is essential, but sales time is vital and it may be necessary to appoint other staff to support the direct sales force.

Customer reception staff are also in the front line and it's important that they are supported not just with training and skills development, but with the technology to make the customer reception process as effective and convenient as possible. The introduction of single points of contact and efficient call transfer has simplified the problem of customer access.

By targeting areas like this where there is immediate and measurable improvement to be made, the company can make significant inroads into customer satisfaction.

- Identify key customer loyalty staff.
- Analyse their customer-facing activities.
- Implement an improvement programme.

59

Introducing recognition and reward

People make an effective contribution when their efforts are recognised and rewarded.

Although incentive and motivation schemes have been operated successfully in direct sales, the schemes have usually been targeted on specific groups and their goals have been short-term. A programme which encourages people to achieve high levels of customer satisfaction must be long-term and must involve more than the sales department.

At senior management level, the programme must relate to overall performance so that managers focus on all the important tasks that affect customer satisfaction. The senior management programme should ideally be cumulative, aiming at continuous improvement over a period of time.

An example is a scheme based on customer survey results. Customers give a rating to dealers or branches on different aspects of the business. The managers achieving the best ratings over a period of time receive a special award.

Employee programmes are more wide-ranging; they need to motivate different groups of employees and to target key groups of people as well. High-visibility programmes which involve the whole company are ideal for focusing attention on the general issue of customer loyalty, but programmes designed to achieve specific results need to be more carefully designed.

An example of a high-visibility programme is one run by a leading car company. The company used a military theme to create high levels of interest. Different departments were designated as platoons and their 'scores' for customer service victories or defeats are added up to earn prizes. Events and displays with a military theme were used to generate interest and involve the whole company.

A campaign built around the TV series *M.A.S.H.* helped to motivate an entire customer service department. Every member of the department was allotted a role in the customer service manoeuvres and the exercise was identified by special uniforms and other insignia which reflected the campaign. Each of the units within the department was given a specific task and the results of the campaigns were measured and shown on a highly visible battle chart.

The results were monitored over a period of time and reported at every level. This helped to keep the participants involved and it also gave opportunities to take corrective action and to focus attention on areas for improvement and development.

Reporting progress

Any programme will fail if people are not kept up to date with progress. Stories abound of companies that fail to notify winning staff of their success in award schemes and of programmes that quickly lose their impetus because nobody is providing continuity.

Any customer loyalty programme should have elements of continuity built into it.

- A magazine which features examples of successful individuals or organisations can act as a prompt and motivates people.
- Letters from senior executives congratulating high achievers and inviting them to participate in an achievement programme will help to maintain interest and motivation.
- Meetings which recognise the achievements of the whole company can help to bring people together and build that vital team spirit.

Summary

Building staff commitment and understanding is an essential part of the customer loyalty process. This chapter explained how to develop the highest levels of commitment by:

61

- creating a customer focused environment to maximise the use of your staff's skills;
- auditing staff understanding to identify awareness and plan customer loyalty communications;
- demonstrating individual contribution to show staff why their actions matter;
- identifying customer expectations so that people are directly aware of the impact of their actions;
- targeting key staff to get the highest performance from staff with the greatest impact on customer loyalty;
- introducing recognition and reward to motivate staff to achieve the highest standards of customer service; and
- reporting progress to maintain the impetus of customer loyalty programmes.

By building the highest levels of staff commitment and understanding, you will ensure that your programmes succeed.

6

Raising customer awareness

Customer care programmes should make customers aware that you are a caring organisation, but you can reinforce the benefits by letting customers know about your commitment. Individual programmes may not demonstrate the full extent of your commitment to customer care and that can prevent the complete success of your programmes.

Contact strategies

How do you maintain contact with your customers between purchases?

A contact strategy allows you to identify all the opportunities and to have a planned approach for every stage. For example, a bank customer might receive an offer of an additional service every time a statement is sent out. This could be a leaflet on insurance services, an offer of a credit card or information on personal loans.

The strategy might be targeted more precisely – it could take high earning customers and offer them high interest savings accounts or gold credit cards or special current accounts with various special options attached to it. By introducing an insurance service and linking it to a home agent system, a bank or any other organisation can increase the level and value of personal contact.

- Can you introduce personal contact into your strategy?
- Can you identify opportunities for contacting your customers more frequently?

- Can you introduce new products or services to increase the frequency of contact?
- Do you incorporate sales messages in every communication with your customers?
- Have you developed a contact strategy for your customers?

Optimising customer contact

Every contact counts. One car manufacturer reckoned to make fifteen million contacts through dealer parts and service departments compared with around a million sales contacts. But if any of those are poor contacts that can adversely affect customer perceptions. For example, late delivery of replacement parts, indifferent service standards or poor handling of complaints can destroy the effectiveness of a customer loyalty programme.

63

Each experience should be a 'customer delight'. It is easy to enrich the customer experience with simple premium gifts or special offers – a free camera with a holiday or a replacement pizza if delivery is late can help to demonstrate care. But far more important is the element of customer care that underpins the whole programme – it is people who make contact with customers and that is where the focus should be. Home delivery staff or insurance collection agents have a superb opportunity to build the highest levels of customer loyalty, but they are not normally regarded as sales people. Yet it is often people like these or the engineers who are working on customer sites who are most trusted by customers and this is where training and support should be focused.

- Where do you have the greatest opportunity to make contact?
- Are the people who make contact trained to deliver a high standard of service?
- How can you support the people who have most contact with customers?

Customer consultation

Some companies use the process of customer consultation in a formal way to build the loyalty of their most important customers. Research and development, for example, provides an opportunity for long-term consultation. An electronics company carries out specific research for a customer and briefs them on future product developments. In that way, they are getting deeply involved in the future of the customer's business.

Where the research programme is more general and likely to benefit all of their customers, they publish consultation documents. Every quarter, they issue details of new products that are planned. Customers are invited to comment on the product or ask for modifications.

Customer user groups or liaison groups fulfil a similar role. Although they are run by small groups of influential people, the majority of customers have an opportunity to express their views through regular meetings. By getting your senior staff involved in user groups, you can demonstrate that you take a positive view of consultation. Consultation ensures that you take account of your customers' views and it also provides the opportunity to maintain regular contact.

- Can you get involved in customers' new product development programmes?
- Do you let customers know about your own direction in research and development?
- Are you involved in industry associations or user groups?

Managing complaints

Dealing effectively with complaints is a very useful way of building customer loyalty. The example set by companies like Marks & Spencer in encouraging customers to return or exchange products if they are not satisfied is in sharp contrast to the defensive walls built by most companies. Marks & Spencer have built a superb reputation for quality and service and this encourages customers to keep coming back. Most leading retailers now have some sort of customer service desk where people can exchange products.

Other companies encourage their customers to complain. They would rather hear the complaints and have an opportunity to put them right than lose business because customers have voted with their feet.

- Do you encourage your customers to complain?
- Do you make it simple for customers to complain?
- Do you have a formal procedure for handling complaints?
- Do you have an improvement programme to deal with the cause of complaints?

65

Customer satisfaction surveys

Customer satisfaction programmes are integral to customer loyalty – they are used to measure the level of satisfaction and highlight areas for improvement.

A survey should ask customers for their views on products and on the standard of service they receive from the company or its distributors. Customers are asked to indicate their degree of satisfaction using a scale such as 'Are you completely satisfied, very satisfied, satisfied, not very satisfied or very dissatisfied?', or 'on a scale of 10, how satisfied were you with . . .? 10 is excellent, 5 is reasonably satisfied, while 2 or less is very poor.'

By issuing a customer satisfaction survey, you demonstrate that your company is serious about customer care. The survey questionnaire should be accompanied by a letter which explains the reasons for the survey and it should invite customers to talk directly to the staff if they have any concerns.

One way of maximising the benefit is to get staff to contact customers directly if they do have concerns and to let customers know what actions have been taken as a result of their comments. This helps to build up two-way communications and shows that the company is responding to customer comments.

When the results of surveys are measured and compared with other dealers or manufacturers, take the opportunity to tell customers about any important achievements. If for example, a distributor achieves an extremely high level of satisfaction and wins an award, let customers know and invite them to take part in the celebrations.

- Which aspect of your product or service should your customers comment on?
- How frequently should you ask your customers for their opinions?
- How do you intend to use the results of the surveys?
- Do you tell customers about your performance in customer satisfaction?
- Do you run a customer satisfaction award scheme for staff?
- Do you have a mechanism for responding to specific customer comments?

Making the most of direct mail

Direct mail is one of the most powerful weapons for building loyalty. Customer information, held on a database, provides the basis for mailings that are precisely targeted at different groups of customers.

The information on a business customer could include:

- size of business;
- main activities;
- number of employees;
- purchasing patterns;
- satisfaction rating; and
- competitor information.

A consumer database might include:

- Occupation and income;
- age;
- family;
- spending patterns; and
- product purchasing history.

The more information you have on your customers, the more precisely you can identify their needs. Direct mail can be used to maintain regular contact and to make specific offers which will appeal to those customers.

For example, direct marketing is used by a pizza company to build initial sales in targeted areas by telling people about introductory offers. When those customers have made their first purchase, the company then mails a series of special offers to encourage repeat purchase and to build their loyalty against competition.

The financial services market is even more sophisticated in its use of direct marketing. Companies know their customers' spending power and they have detailed personal profiles which enable them to target specific financial products.

- Are you making the most of your customer information?
- Can you use surveys, questionnaires or other forms of enquiry to improve the quality of your customer information?
- Have you got a planned programme for mailing loyalty building offers?

Integrating customer loyalty into all your communications

Customer loyalty messages should not be communicated in isolation – they form an integral part of all marketing communications. The message might be as simple as 'we care for our customers' or 'everything we do is driven by you' or 'we are a caring company', or it may be a more specific message such as 'we have

67

now extended our opening hours' or 'we've moved to a new site with even more parking and we've given you even more choice'.

- Do you have a policy statement on customer loyalty issues?
- Do you include information on service or product improvements in your communications?
- Do you take every opportunity to remind customers that you want to build their loyalty?

Summary

Although customer loyalty programmes should demonstrate to customers that you are a caring organisation, you can reinforce the benefits of the programmes by operating a positive customer communications programme. This chapter explained the key elements of this:

- developing a contact strategy to maintain effective planned contact with customers;
- optimising customer contact by making sure that every form of contact creates the right impression and builds loyalty;
- carrying out customer consultation to get involved in your customers' business;
- managing complaints to demonstrate that you care about your customers' concerns;
- carrying out customer satisfaction surveys to measure satisfaction and build two-way communications;
- making the most of direct mail to maintain regular contact with targeted customers; and
- integrating customer loyalty into all your communications.

These supporting communications help to ensure the complete success of your customer loyalty programmes.

7

Providing staff with skills

Defining staff contribution

The previous chapter showed how the development of commitment and understanding are essential stages in equipping staff to build customer loyalty. But, unless staff have the skills to make a contribution, that commitment could be wasted. Training is an essential element of the customer loyalty process, but it should operate at two levels – at a generic level where people learn basic customer care skills – and at the specific level where people are trained in the customer care activities relevant to their own jobs.

The first stage is to make a grid of all the people whose actions will affect customer loyalty and to rank their contribution in terms of its importance. A comprehensive list might include:

- sales;
- distribution;
- manufacturing;
- design/development;
- marketing;
- communications;
- personnel;
- training;
- purchasing;
- customer service;

- quality; and
- administration.

Against this list it is possible to plot the key customer loyalty tasks.

- Look at Chapter 2 (Allocating responsibility for customer loyalty) to check what these should be.
- Measure performance against defined quality standards. This enables a benchmark to be set for future performance and improvement.
- Document the tasks and standards so that people are aware of their responsibilities and so that the key tasks can be managed effectively.

Identifying training needs

Training needs are linked to the individual customer loyalty contribution that each member of staff makes. By identifying the key performance characteristics needed for success, the company can plan its training programme and help people to make the best possible contribution to customer needs.

Training programmes can also be linked to the results of customer satisfaction surveys. By identifying trends in performance and customer requirements, training can be focused on critical areas.

- If customers feel that they need support for their own operations, the training programme will focus on project management or supervisory skills, rather than technical skills.
- If the customer decides that his own staff performance needs to be improved, the training emphasis will be on presentation and training skills.
- If clients identify a level of dissatisfaction with the service, then it is more important that training concentrates on the technical skills needed to operate to higher standards.

  In this situation, training analysis is too important to be left to the training department. It needs the co-operation of people in sales, marketing, quality and customer service to ensure that the customer's real needs are being met.

Integrating training with customer care

Product training and personal skills development should not be separated from the development of customer care skills – they are all integrated. Some companies are redefining their technical training programmes as customer care programmes on the basis that customer satisfaction and loyalty are directly related to the successful performance of key tasks. Technical training, for example, has as its main objectives the successful repair of a customer's product – trained staff deliver a higher quality of service and customers should return for more.

Product training ensures that sales staff will be able to demonstrate a better understanding of a product and its application to a customer's problems. The customer gets the best possible solution and that leads to higher levels of satisfaction.

Personal skills development is essential to the delivery of a quality service:

- recruit people who are motivated to succeed through achievement;
- put staff through continuous specialist and quality training programmes to develop their own personal skills; and
- ensure that staff understand your requirements for the highest standards of service.

Management skills

It is not just the staff who need the skills to deliver a quality service, the process of customer loyalty must be managed properly for effective results. Managers must be able to

71

communicate customer loyalty to their staff and build their commitment, so management training must focus on presentation and communication skills.

Summary

Staff training is an essential part of the customer loyalty process – ensuring that staff have the skills to make an effective contribution. This chapter explained how the process could be managed by:

- defining staff contribution and measuring their performance against customer loyalty standards;
- identifying training needs to ensure that it is focused on critical areas;
- integrating training with customer care to develop personal skills that will build customer loyalty; and
- improving management skills to ensure that customer loyalty is effectively managed.

By identifying the key performance characteristics needed for success, you can plan an effective training programme.

8

Building partnership

Why partnership is important

Partnership is a term that describes a business relationship between a company and its customers or suppliers. It is a relationship in which companies co-operate formally or informally in areas critical to the customer's business performance. Partnership also tends to reduce the element of competition because of closer co-operation between supplier and customer. The customer enjoys security of supply, as well as continuity of contact and consistent quality.

Partnership typically leads to closer working relationships between companies – the customer shares his or her business objectives and the supplier provides services that are dedicated to the customer. The supplier provides the customer with information on his or her own forward plans so that the two can integrate their product developments.

Partnership is an increasingly important issue because companies are becoming mutually dependent and are able to make effective use of each other's skills and resources. For example, many companies are now sourcing non-essential services outside the company so that they can concentrate on their core business. By allowing key staff to concentrate on essential tasks the company can achieve business objectives more rapidly while a specialist company provides non-essential service more cost effectively.

The shortage of skilled staff is another factor behind partnership.

By using specialists, the company does not have to hire or retrain other staff.

The influence of technology can create closer working relationships. For example, the manufacturing technology of JIT (Just-In-Time) requires closer co-operation between manufacturer and supplier to ensure that the material required for manufacturing is available when it is needed. The information technology which supports JIT becomes an integral part of both manufacturers' and suppliers' operations and that encourages partnership.

Partnership opportunities

Look at your existing customer list for partnership opportunities and analyse current business levels as well as competitive activity.

- Would your customers benefit from consistency of quality or delivery?
- What is the purchasing pattern?
- Would a more formal purchasing arrangement provide the customer with benefits?
- Are your services essential to your customers' long-term business success?
- Are your clients introducing new technology – they will need long-term support to make the most of the technology.
- Do your clients regularly run recruitment advertisements for skilled staff – can you support them by providing those skills?

Changing relationships

Partnership requires a continuous communications effort to sustain the new relationship, but there's a significant change in the relationship because the company is likely to be dealing at many different levels.

Traditional sales activity was focused on the purchasing department, but partnership involves many more people on both the client and supplier side.

- Identify the key personnel involved in partnership, beginning at the top. Partnership should be presented as part of a strategic initiative because it helps a company meet its business objectives more effectively.

- Brief senior executives on the implications and benefits of partnership for their business. They must be committed to making it work because partnership involves trust and co-operation, as well as the sharing of confidential information.

- Communicate the changing relationships between supplier and client to build understanding and show how partnership will work in practice.

- Introduce a continuing communications programme to keep both parties up to date with developments in the two organisations.

Changing sales force attitudes

The sales force is key to the success of partnership, but their role must change.

- Explain why they have to adopt a longer-term perspective, and look at future relationships rather than just short-term sales potential.

- Introduce training in managing customer relationships.

- Encourage sales staff to sell services which support high-value capital equipment. Services add value to a product but, because they represent lower turnover than the main product range, they may be seen as time-consuming activity which does not offer any significant rewards.

- Restructure the sales force incentive package to reflect the importance of customer loyalty activities.

75

■ Provide the sales force with the information and support material they need to give customers the right level of service.

Managing account relationships

Partnership depends on the effective management of relationships at many different levels. These relationships should be formally identified and used as the basis of a relationship programme.

Relationship marketing is used to ensure that each of the key contacts in a partnership holds the right perceptions of your company. Customers should recognise that they are getting added value and that partnership is essential to their business success.

Account relationships can be influence, not just by personal contact, but by direct and indirect communications.

■ Identify what each member of the partnership team needs to know and set up formal communications channels to ensure that information is carefully targeted.

■ Audit the communications to ensure they convey the key messages and positioning statements that the company needs to get across.

■ Set up a formal procedure for meetings and consultation to increase the level of effective contact.

Contribution of services

Services are essential to the development of partnership. They provide an opportunity to maintain constant relationships and they add value to products.

■ Use life-cycle analysis and other prospecting techniques to identify where services might be needed.

■ Use consultancy services to develop a deep understanding of

the client's business objectives so that future service developments can be matched to customer needs.

- Look at the client's own support operations and develop a
  business case which analyses the cost and time involved in
  providing those services internally.

- Put together a presentation which demonstrates the cost-
  effectiveness of using external services.

Adding value

Partnership can help customers enhance their own business performance by adding value. For example, by gaining access to skills
not available inside his own company, the customer can improve
activities that provide a competitive edge.

For example, by inviting a customer's senior executives to a series
of strategy seminars, the supplier can build their loyalty because
they are enhancing their own skills and improving their company's decision-making capabilities.

Added value solutions are vital to partnership because they
demonstrate that the client is getting real value for money out of
the relationship.

Meeting customers' changing requirements

Partnership is a long-term relationship so it is important to
understand the customer's changing business requirements. This
can be achieved by working at a consultative level with the company's senior management team.

It is also important to encourage feedback on the quality of product and service provided. This shows that the supplier is concerned about quality and that it is responsive to customer needs.

Summary

Partnership is an extreme form of customer loyalty in which customer and supplier work closely together to achieve mutual benefits such as security of supply and continuity of contact. To build and maintain partnership takes a sustained management effort to:

- identify partnership opportunities by analysing your customers' business activities;
- understand and develop the changing relationships between customer and supplier through a continuous communications programme;
- change sales force attitudes to ensure they build relationships rather than just sell products;
- manage account relationships so that customers recognise partnership as essential to their business success;
- use services to maintain contact and add value;
- add value by enhancing your customers' skills; and
- meet customers' changing requirements by working closely with the customer team.

Through partnership you can build closer relationships with your customers and reduce the impact of competitive activity.

Part II

■

CUSTOMER LOYALTY
IN ACTION

The first part of this book explained the management actions required to build customer loyalty. The next part demonstrates customer loyalty programmes in action in a variety of different market sectors:

- service;
- the oil business;
- components market;
- travel;
- consultancy and professional services;
- information systems;
- car market;
- financial services; and
- retail.

These sectors have been chosen to reflect business conditions that apply in many other sectors. Although the case histories may seem specific, the action lists recommend activities that can be universally applied.

9

Winning with service

Supporting your customers' business with service

An independent service company does not have its own customer base as a foundation for the business. It has to win customers from the original equipment supplier, or from its competitors. While the most effective strategy for entering the market and gaining business is price, this is not an effective means of building long-term loyalty. Original equipment manufacturers understand that service loyalty is critical to their own customer loyalty. They need to retain customer loyalty between product sales to ensure the next sale, so they are putting an increasing emphasis on the quality of their service operations. But, when an independent service organisation has no products of its own, how can it build customer loyalty?

DEVELOPING A CUSTOMISED SERVICE PACKAGE

A company specialising in servicing domestic electrical goods carries out a significant amount of sub-contract work for a number of high street electrical retailers. The retailers offer customers the manufacturers' warranty in the first year of ownership, and then market their own service plan for the next two years, using the specialist subcontractor.

Although this gives the service organisation a certain continuity of work, their success depends on how effectively the retailer markets service. They are also at risk if the manufacturer decides to extend his own warranty and service operations to maintain control. The company approaches a television rental company with a proposal to develop a special rental package that will cover a broad range of electrical goods not normally available through rental agreements.

BUILDING DEPENDENCE ON YOUR SERVICE

This proposal will build partnership and loyalty in a number of ways. The service element is an integral part of the package from day one, so the service organisation has continuity of work throughout the period of rental agreement. The cost of service is included in the customer payment so future service revenue is not dependent on customer choice. It also builds partnership with the direct customer – the rental company. The service company has helped the retailer to develop his own business by providing an added value service to customers. The service company provides the skills, resources and infrastructure to deliver the service, so the rental company does not have to make any investment. It also helps the rental company develop its own competitive edge by offering customers greater choice, flexibility and service. The service organisation has moved from the position of supplier providing service on demand to the status of a business partner, essential to the success of the customer's business.

BUILDING THE RELATIONSHIP

Targeted communications will ensure the success of this initiative. The proposal to the rental company must convince them that the service company can deliver consistent, quality service to their customers. The proposal – in the form of a slide presentation with accompanying documentation – outlines the business benefits of the package and explains why the service company has the resources and skills to handle the work cost-effectively. It explains how the service will be delivered and lays down quality standards.

D

TELLING CONSUMERS ABOUT THE SERVICE

While television and video rental is well-established, the concept of rental for other electrical goods such as washing machines, dishwashers and stereo systems is unfamiliar. Consumers need to be convinced that they will benefit from this new arrangement. The communications stress the long-term care they will enjoy, the continued reliability of their equipment, and the flexibility with which they can replace products. This presents rental as far more flexible and lower in overall cost than outright purchase. It sells the concept and builds loyalty to the rental company.

ACTION

▶ **Do you depend on other people for your customers?**

▶ **If you handle sub-contract work, can you use quality to build customer loyalty?**

▶ **Can you improve the quality of service your customers offer?**

▶ **Can you handle specific operations for your customers cost effectively?**

Providing customers with a single source of service

The computer industry demonstrates an opportunity that may be widespread in other business sectors. Developments in computer networks and communications mean that companies now have a much wider choice of computer equipment. They can select products from a number of different suppliers and tailor the best system to meet their business requirements.

SIMPLIFYING COMPLEX SERVICING

Equipment standards organisations have developed open systems standards which help manufacturers integrate their equipment with other systems. The customer benefits from having the widest choice of equipment but this choice increases the complexity of service. Traditionally, each piece of equipment was serviced and maintained by the original supplier – there was really no choice. But when one site has equipment from six or more suppliers – these are known as multi-vendor sites – the problems of service co-ordination multiply. The company support staff have to contact a number of different specialists with queries, and it can be difficult to work out the cause of a fault, particularly if it affects several pieces of equipment. Suppliers naturally blame each other in that situation – a problem known as fingerpointing. Obtaining service on multi-vendor sites is time-consuming, expensive, complex and frustrating.

PROVIDING A SINGLE SOURCE

Service organisations are responding to this by co-ordinating the service of all manufacturers' equipment. They offer the service in a variety of ways – either by managing the various specialists from different suppliers or by delivering the service themselves.

THE COST ARGUMENTS FOR SINGLE-SOURCE SERVICE

Convincing customers that single-source service is a benefit is an important part of the communications process. The first stage is to convince customers that it is cost-effective. The service company looks closely at the direct cost of services and also the indirect cost of administering traditional services from many different sources. Other cost factors such as loss of efficiency or poor service to users can also be built into the cost equation. The service company demonstrate this best by preparing individual case studies which analyse the cost of service and potential savings. At the end of the study, the service company offers to carry out an audit of the service and support operations and use the results as a basis for making a single-source service recommendation.

MANAGING THE QUALITY OF THE SERVICE

That approach can be used to convince a customer that single-source service is the right route, but the company also has to persuade them that they are in the best position to deliver that service. The service company explains that it has the skills and resources to offer a range of solutions.

ENSURING QUALITY

If it is delivering the service by managing other specialists, it is essential to demonstrate the management processes that will be used to control the service. Conformance to British Standards, for example, tells customers that the service will be delivered to the highest standards of quality. Written service descriptions reassure customers that all aspects of service will be to the same standards.

SETTING UP THE RIGHT INFRASTRUCTURE

Fault diagnosis is an essential aspect of efficient service; the service company should explain how it uses diagnostics or other service routines to analyse faults rapidly and get the right solution. Spares are also critical to service standards, particularly when the stock has to cover such a wide variety of equipment. The company has to show how it will manage the sourcing of spares and delivery so that there are no hold-ups. If the company is going to deliver all the service itself, it has to show it has the skills to handle this. It can either build up a team of quality-controlled subcontractors or it can use its own staff who have undergone special training to deal with a very broad range of equipment.

STRENGTHENING RELATIONSHIPS

Single-source service is a valuable way to build partnership with a customer. Because the service supplier handles all the equipment service on a site, he understands how the customer uses information systems to achieve business benefits. He is then in a position to make further recommendations on future investments. The service company can also demonstrate how it is helping the customer make the best use of his own resources and equipment. By working in partnership, the two can establish how to achieve the best business benefits.

ACTION

- ▶ **Do your customers use equipment from a number of different sources?**
- ▶ **Are they able to co-ordinate different sources of service efficiently?**
- ▶ **Have you carried out an analysis of the cost of your customers' support operations?**
- ▶ **Are you able to identify savings by providing a single-source of service?**
- ▶ **Do you have the skills and resources to provide single source service yourself?**
- ▶ **Do you have the quality control systems and the management skills to co-ordinate the work of other subcontractors?**

85

Integrating service with a customer's business

A service organisation is often judged by its ability to respond to a service request or to carry out an effective repair. But, this does not help to build customer loyalty in the long term. The service is reactive and does not represent value to the customer. Service and repairs are an additional cost and customers often resent paying for them.

DEALING WITH PRICE COMPETITION

In some businesses, routine service can be reduced to a commodity and an efficient organisation can lose business to a low-price competitor. While many companies seek to build their service business by securing service contracts, they frequently cover only basic requirements, they are negotiated on an annual basis and they are price-sensitive with little opportunity to achieve high margins or differentiate the service.

A company specialising in factory maintenance is considering ways of building the long-term strength of its business and improving profitability. It currently has a wide range of contracts covering different aspects of factory maintenance, but it faces strong competition on a number of sites.

DIFFERENTIATING THE SERVICE

The maintenance company analyses the pattern of its business and identifies an opportunity to develop planned maintenance programmes for customers. Planned maintenance is a method of integrating a number of separate service and maintenance activities so that they can be handled more efficiently. The key to success in planned maintenance is the development of a mainten-ance database in which all activities are entered and analysed to produce a schedule which can be fine-tuned to develop the best possible maintenance programme. The programme can then be compared with sales and production schedules to ensure that maintenance does not take place during a busy production period. The maintenance company worked closely with a computer soft-ware consultancy to develop programmes that would allow it to evaluate its own maintenance information and integrate the information with customers.

TAILORING THE SERVICE

The company was then able to develop a number of specific pro-posals to show customers how they could achieve savings and improve the efficiency of their factory. The maintenance company was able to demonstrate added value and this justified the rela-tively higher cost of the service. The planned maintenance pack-age included an element of consultancy and project management to ensure that the plan was tailored to the needs of the factory. The plan included regular service on all equipment, phased to make use of shut-downs, holidays or quiet periods. The company provided an emergency standby service and kept an agreed level of spares so that there were no delays in routine service or emergency calls.

ADDING VALUE TO THE SERVICE

In presenting its arguments to customers, the maintenance company stressed the improvement in efficiency that was likely to occur, provided planned maintenance was part of an integrated approach to manufacturing. By developing a fully costed plan that was integrated with customers' manufacturing programmes, the company was able to add value to a basic service and differentiate itself from price competitors.

ACTION

▶ **Can your service be differentiated or is it a commodity service?**

▶ **Do you use your customers' business patterns to develop your own service programmes?**

▶ **Can your service programmes be managed on a regular basis?**

▶ **Can you charge higher prices for an added value service?**

87

Keeping maintenance business by introducing higher standards of service

A computer company wants to build greater account control through its service activities. It understands that service is the key to maintaining contact between major systems sales, but its traditional service business is threatened by lower cost competitors who are winning contracts for the simplest forms of maintenance. One competitor has stepped up the pace of the attack by allocating engineers who remain on a customer site on a continuous basis. They are in regular contact with customer staff and they are able to influence many factors, including the direction of future purchases.

USING NEW TECHNOLOGY TO MAINTAIN AN EDGE

The computer company does not have the resources to allocate engineers to all of its customer sites, nor does it believe that this is an effective use of resources. The company believes that one engineer would not have the skills to handle diagnosis and repair on the complex installations at any of its customer sites. Its preferred solution is to invest in sophisticated diagnostics which enables it to maintain equipment remotely and analyse faults before an engineer goes on site. These diagnostic links help to provide a better service to customers by ensuring that there is minimal delay before equipment is repaired. When an engineer does go on site, he is fully prepared with a diagnosis and with the right spares.

USING SERVICE INFORMATION TO IMPROVE QUALITY

Remote service poses one problem for the company in that customers do not always recognise the speed or quality of response. Because so much of the process is automated, the customer may not be aware of a problem. The term 'remote' is unfriendly and in contrast to the image of the personal service representative on site. However, diagnostics do prove to be a powerful form of account control. The information available from the diagnostic system allows the service company to build up a detailed service database which can be used to plan future service programmes and identify opportunities for new service business.

The service company is able to use that database information to provide valuable technical advice and guidance to customers and make recommendations on support levels. By using this information in a positive way, the company can build partnership with its customers. It also reassures customers who are increasing their use of computers that the service company will be able to handle more complex requirements in the long term.

PROVIDING CUSTOMERS WITH CENTRES OF EXCELLENCE

When the service company presents its new support strategy to customers, it presents the long-term benefits of diagnostics — showing how support can be simplified and enhanced, and how their equipment will be used in a more cost-effective way. The presentation stresses the positive benefits and shows how the service company's engineering skills can be used to full effect. By grouping people and systems into centres of excellence, the service company can deliver the best service for its customers and build up an expertise that will be of real long-term value.

ACTION

► **Can you overcome price competition by increasing the quality of your service?**

► **Can you use sophisticated service tools to give yourself a competitive edge?**

► **Are you using service information to build your future service plans?**

► **Do you stress the cost-effectiveness of your investment in service technology?**

89

Improving the response to service queries

When a customer needs help, he usually wants it quickly. It may be a domestic emergency, or it may be an equipment problem which threatens the efficiency of a business. Sometimes a company cannot provide help immediately but, by giving the customer a clear indication that help is on its way, it can provide the reassurance that is crucial to customer satisfaction and loyalty.

PROVIDING REASSURANCE

Psychologists, working in the field of customer service, have found that customers are willing to wait reasonable lengths of time for a solution to their problem, provided they are kept informed of progress and reassured that action is taking place. This can give service companies considerably more flexibility in their operations. By maintaining an effective level of contact with their customers, they can allocate resources to meet the most urgent requirements, rather than attempting to deal with every call as soon as it happens.

MAKING CONTACT EASIER

It is also important to make it easy for customers to get in touch with the right department. A service company wants to simplify the process of contact for customers and build the highest levels of customer satisfaction. It sets up a national customer centre where customers can ring one number to place all service requests to get advice or assistance on other service matters. This replaced the existing system of more than ten numbers for different types of service. Customers found they were being asked to ring different numbers and getting varied response, depending on where they were located.

IMPROVING THE QUALITY OF RESPONSE

Now customers had only to ring one number and their request was routed to the right location. The staff at the customer service centre took responsibility for contacting the right specialists and they then called the customer back to confirm the arrangements. They also took the opportunity to impose consistent standards for response and call-back to ensure the customer received a quality service. Customers could feel confident that they were getting a high standard of service, and they also enjoyed simpler service administration, allowing them to concentrate on more important tasks.

BUILDING THE INFRASTRUCTURE

Behind this service initiative was a broad-ranging communications programme aimed at the people who delivered the service as well as the customers who benefited from it. It was essential that staff understood their role in the new system because, without their commitment, the initiative could fail. A series of present-ations was given to departmental or local branch managers to explain their contribution to customer response. For example, some local branches had provided their own response to requests and had taken pride in their own standards of service. The local service departments had to feel that they were not losing a sense of identity, but were gaining a more important role that was central to the success of the company. Training would also be critical to the success of the new venture, so a training guide was developed which would enable each member of staff to make the most effective contribution to the success of the operation.

HELPING CUSTOMERS MAKE THE MOST OF THE SERVICE

Customer communications were important. Although customers were formally notified of the new arrangements, it was essential that they also understood the benefits. Groups of information systems directors were invited to the customer service centre to see the service at first hand. An introductory brochure explained the concept and the technology behind the approach, while bulletins kept customers up to date with the project. The company also took the opportunity to brief customers on the best way to use the customer service centre. Requests for service had sometimes been delayed by customer staff unable to provide adequate information on the problem or the query. A brief customer guide ensured that both parties understood what was required of them.

91

ACTION

► **Do you make it easy for customers to contact you when they need help?**

► **Can you provide a single point of access to simplify contact?**

► **Do you have to respond immediately to calls for assistance or can you plan a response that recognises customer priorities?**

► **Do you tell your customers how to make the best use of your services?**

► **Do your staff understand their role in the response mechanism?**

Maintaining customer relationships with long-term service plans

Most manufacturers provide their customers with at least one year's guarantee on a new product. Others may wish to extend that guarantee into a second year, provided the customer has the product maintained in line with recommended service schedules. But, it is common for customers then to neglect servicing beyond the second year on the basis that they do not have to meet warranty requirements. Manufacturers and their dealers lose service revenue and they also lose the opportunity to influence customer loyalty.

HELPING CUSTOMERS IMPROVE RELIABILITY

An electrical maintenance contractor saw the opportunity to build its own service business by providing long-term service contracts for one of its industrial customers – a manufacturer of machine tools. The manufacturer had a reputation for delivering quality products, but lack of effective maintenance was giving his customers reliability problems in later years. Competitors were exploiting this situation and introducing longer warranty periods to enhance their own reputations. That combination of reliability and low price was giving the competitors a clear edge in the marketplace and helping them build market share. The contractor put together a proposal that would help the manufacturer regain the lead in reliability.

BUILDING THE LONG-TERM RELATIONSHIP

Their proposal covered a five-year period. In the first two years, they handled scheduled service work on behalf of the manufacturer. They built up a database of customers and maintained service history files. Any warranty work was covered under the manufacturer's normal terms and the service organisation reclaimed the cost of any repairs. They used the customer database to set up a direct marketing programme which enabled them to contact customers as they were approaching the end of the warranty. The customers were offered a choice of three- or five-year plans which provided an extended warranty backed by a priority repair service.

MAINTAINING THE QUALITY OF THE SERVICE

The contractor charged the customer a structured service fee, but included in the package a range of service benefits such as four-hour emergency cover, a replacement service for essential equipment and a re-manufacturing service for older equipment. The contractor built up his own service expertise by enhancing the service database with information on all the service calls and it was able to develop a telephone helpline service to help customers diagnose faults. The service records also provided valuable customer information which was used to improve the quality of customer response. When a customer contacted the contractor with a query, all the information on product, location and service history was available, and the receptionist was able to offer a rapid informed response.

IMPROVING THE CUSTOMER'S BUSINESS PERFORMANCE

This level of service helped to build partnership with customers. The customer was now dependent on the service supplier and the expertise he had developed. If other service organisations wanted to compete for the manufacturer's business, they would be starting a long way behind; they might be able to compete on price, but they would not be able to deliver the high level of service. The service contractor was able to offer the manufacturer other benefits of partnership. First and foremost was the improved levels of reliability which increased satisfaction among the manufacturer's customers. The improved levels of reliability reflected well on the quality of the manufacturer's products and this helped future sales opportunities. With major investment programmes occurring every five to six years, the manufacturer was able to maintain contact throughout the buying cycle. He was also able to draw on the service information supplied by the service organisation to identify sales opportunities and get feedback on the performance of the equipment.

MAINTAINING THE RELATIONSHIP

In presenting the initial proposal to the manufacturer, the service contractor stressed the potential benefits of the partnership – the service expertise the customer would obtain and the long-term benefits of customer loyalty. In this way, the service contractor was able to differentiate itself from other service companies and position itself as a business partner, rather than just a supplier. It maintained a consistent communications programme to keep manufacturers up to date with enhancements to the service and to sell more of the higher value services. As well as the service, it also stressed the benefits of the improved reception process and the helpline which provided a rapid response to service requirements.

ACTION

- ▶ **Can you improve your customers' business performance by supplementing their service resources?**
- ▶ **Do warranty periods give you the opportunity to increase contact with your customers?**
- ▶ **Are you using service information to develop a customer information service?**
- ▶ **Can you use the service relationship to build partnership?**

Matching the level of service to your customers' needs

Customers expect quality when they buy service, but quality is relative; it should meet the customers' requirements and it should meet certain pre-defined standards. One of the problems facing any service organisation is what level to pitch the quality of its service. If it is too high, it may be too expensive or too elaborate for some customers. But, if it is too low, customers may not think standards are sufficient. Pitching service quality at a single level can also limit the amount of business that an organisation can handle.

ANALYSING SERVICE LEVEL REQUIREMENTS

A contractor analysed the service it was offering and carried out telephone research to establish service products and the buying factors that customers thought were most important. This helped the contractor build up a profile of its customer base and identified the key requirements for future development. The contractor found that many of the factors it thought important had little appeal for customers and they modified the service to reflect the findings.

OFFERING A STRUCTURED SERVICE

The major benefit of the survey was the service pattern that emerged. Customer requirements fell into three distinct groups and these mirrored the levels of service the company was able to offer. As a result, the contractor decided to modify the way it delivered service. Customers were now offered a structured service from which they would choose a level that was most appropriate to their needs.

95

THE EMERGENCY SERVICE

The most basic service was not a budget service, but a no-frills service for customers who had an internal service department. This type of customer only needed support in emergencies or when support tasks were too large for the internal team. However, because they depended on their machinery the customers wanted to be sure of a rapid response to their service requests and the right level of cover.

THE COMPREHENSIVE SERVICE

The most comprehensive service was aimed at companies with no internal support operation or no service experience with a particular type of product. This service included equipment installation and training, scheduled maintenance, emergency repairs and a telephone hotline which provided equipment users with advice and guidance. An optional service management training module was also included which helped the customer develop his own support expertise.

THE STANDARD SERVICE

The standard service offered customers the most popular range of services. It was packaged to appeal to the widest possible range of customers and it included elements that would have broad market appeal. High levels of service and maintenance, flexible response times and additional support services ensured that this represented the best value for money. The standard service was the nearest equivalent to the original level of service and it was priced to offer the most competitive package.

DIFFERENTIATING THE SERVICE

The emergency and comprehensive services helped to broaden the appeal and also enabled the contractor to compete in niche markets where it was not previously seen as a serious contender. In the comprehensive sector, for example, it was able to offer a premium service and charge higher rates to customers who demanded higher standards. In areas where customers needed additional skills and expertise, the contractor was able to demonstrate higher value and this helped to differentiate it from competitors. The contractor was able to show that, although its prices were higher, the service elements included in a contract provided long-term benefits and therefore represented greater overall value.

SEGMENTING THE MARKET

The contractor used direct marketing to communicate with targeted prospects in the three different sectors. The customer survey helped to pinpoint key customer groups and the information formed the basis of targeted direct marketing. In its direct mail, the contractor stressed the comprehensive nature of its services and showed how it could deliver the right solution to its customers' service needs. The contractor is providing more than maintenance – it is helping customers to run their own business more efficiently. The direct mail explains each of the services in detail and includes scenarios which explain how the services can be used.

MAINTAINING CUSTOMER RELATIONSHIPS

Structured service helps to maintain customer loyalty by providing customers with the right level of service and allowing them to move into another level of service if their support needs change. To maintain that contact and build the element of partnership, the contractor carries out annual audits and consultancy on service requirements. These help the customer understand changing service needs in relation to the business and it demonstrates that the service contractor is concerned with long-term business issues and not just maintenance.

ACTION

► **Can you differentiate customers' service needs?**

► **Do you need to develop different levels of service offer?**

► **Do you survey your customers' needs and analyse the information?**

► **Can you increase the levels of flexibility customers enjoy?**

Improving convenience for customers

Customer loyalty is vital to an insurance company. Customers buy many different insurance-related products during their lifetime, and a general insurance company has a unique opportunity to build a high level of repeat business – motor insurance, household insurance, endowment and savings policies, mortgage endowment policies, retirement pensions and health insurance. Increasingly, insurance companies have an opportunity to sell a broader range of financial services, so the concept of 'customers for life' should be integral to their whole business. Household insurance is just one part of the business, but this example shows how added-value services can help to retain and win customers.

MEETING CHANGING COMPETITION

People buy household insurance in a number of ways – direct from an insurance company, through a financial adviser or broker acting as agent for a number of insurance companies, or as part of the mortgage package offered by a lender such as a building society or bank. Although, traditionally, few customers had moved their policies, increasing competition between banks, building societies, insurance companies and other financial institutions has broken the traditional links and forced the insurance companies to look more closely at their products and services. Customer research showed that premium levels and terms were important, but quality of service also played a crucial role in the choice of insurers.

DIFFERENTIATING THE SERVICE

The research showed that there were two opportunities to improve customer satisfaction and loyalty – first, by ensuring that a higher proportion of customers renewed their premiums and, second, by encouraging customers to pay higher premiums for different levels of service. One widely adopted method of improving customer service is to set up a helpline which customers can use in emergencies to get information, advice or help. Research showed that, in an emergency, people wanted to know that their problems could be resolved. Domestic incidents such as fires, burst pipes, floods or burglary caused a great deal of personal distress, and it is reassuring that personal help and professional assistance is available at the end of a telephone. A helpline service adds value to a policy and helps to differentiate a company from its competitors.

PROVIDING DIFFERENT LEVELS OF SERVICE

Helplines like these provide several different levels of service. The first level covers advice and guidance on what to do in an emergency so that customers can take remedial action and contact the right people. A second level of help allows customers to register a claim immediately by telephone. An insurance assessor then calls to make an assessment and settle the claim quickly so that customers can begin to take remedial action. A third element is a directory of local emergency services so that customers can have repairs carried out by competent specialists. According to research, customers believed that, in an emergency, they would be at the mercy of unscrupulous suppliers who could do a hurried job and charge an unfair price.

MAINTAINING THE QUALITY OF SERVICE

99

To ensure that their customers receive a quality service, a number of insurance companies have set up a register of approved emergency contractors such as plumbers, builders and electricians. The contractors have to achieve specified standards of workmanship, operate an agreed scale of charges and maintain minimum response times so that customers are assured of a prompt service. Their performance is monitored by the insurance companies to ensure that they continue to provide the highest standards of service.

MAINTAINING RELATIONSHIPS WITH SERVICE SUPPLIERS

The quality of service to customers depends on the quality of local contractors. Insurance companies operate separate communications programmes to attract contractors and implement the service standards. Introductory mailers offer local contractors the opportunity to reach specified standards and become approved suppliers. The mailers explain the business opportunities and the investment the insurance company is making in quality service. The insurance company may also help a local contractor to invest in the right sort of equipment and improve the quality of service.

An operating manual lays down precise guidelines on the standards of service that should be delivered.

PROVIDING A CONSISTENT NATIONWIDE SERVICE

This controlled franchise arrangement benefited the insurance companies, the contractors and the policy holders, providing excellent opportunities to build effective relationships. Contractors, for example, get more opportunities for business and enhance their professional status; they can trade as approved contractors and use this to build other business. The insurance companies can build a national network without a great deal of investment by making use of existing suppliers. Customers get a consistent, quality local service, wherever they are in the country.

STRUCTURING THE SERVICE

Customers do not have to make a number of different phone calls, they simply dial one number at local rates and the insurance company makes the appropriate contacts. On some policies, each caller is appointed a personal incident manager who provides an individual service and maintains contact until the end of an incident. The helpline service can be structured in a number of ways to reflect the needs and expectations of different groups of customers. Structuring the service helps companies segment the market and develop specialist policies that are precisely targeted at specific sectors. For example, customers who subscribe to the higher level of service would also receive a local directory with special subscriber information on the national network, as well as a guide to the services available. The services can be further differentiated by branding, for example gold service, or all-star service. This helps to add further value to the policy and reinforce customer loyalty.

MAINTAINING CONTACT WITH CUSTOMERS

Existing policy holders are informed of the service through a direct-marketing programme, while national television and press advertising are used to attract new prospects. Direct marketing enables the insurance company to maintain regular contact with their customers and segment the market by targeting different levels of service. Customer literature is used to explain the services; it provides useful hints on what to do in an emergency, as well as the telephone numbers and contacts appropriate to the level of service. Customer follow-up, such as a questionnaire or courtesy telephone call after an incident, can also help to build customer satisfaction and reinforce the relationship.

A service like this builds customer loyalty because it shows a caring attitude to the customer at a time of potential personal distress. It is also a logical extension to an insurance policy, providing a complete insurance and recovery service. It adds value to the basic product, builds high levels of customer satisfaction, demonstrates customer care and encourages customer loyalty.

101

ACTION

► **Can you sell additional products to your customer base as their needs change?**

► **Do you support the concept of 'customers for life'?**

► **Can you use service to differentiate your products?**

► **Can you offer different levels of service to attract incremental income and segment the market?**

► **If you use other people to deliver a customer service, can you control the quality of their service?**

► **Do you make it easy for your customers to contact you?**

► **Can you introduce added-value services which demonstrate customer care?**

► **Have you got a regular customer base?**

Summary

The service sector demonstrates how services can be used to build customer loyalty. It also shows that services can be differentiated in a number of ways to add value to customer relationships and reduce the impact of competition. The key actions include:

- supporting your customers' business with service so that they depend on you;
- providing customers with a single source of service to simplify their administration, offer consistency and quality and strengthen relationships;
- integrating your service with a customer's business to differentiate a commodity service and increase dependence;
- introducing higher standards of service to maintain an edge over price competitors;
- improving the response to service queries to make it easier for customers to buy from you;
- maintaining customer relationships with long-term service plans;
- matching the level of service to your customers' needs to segment the market and improve customer relationships; and
- improving convenience for customers to demonstrate the highest levels of customer care.

Service developments like these can be applied to any market sector where after-sales services are important.

10

The oil business

Oil competes with gas and electricity as a domestic and industrial fuel; it is the raw material for processors in the petrochemical industry; and it is at the heart of the road transport business. Oil companies face competition within their own industry, as well as from other energy suppliers, and the drive to build customer loyalty operates at a number of different levels. As the examples show, there are few opportunities to differentiate the product – it is the level of service which wins and retains customers.

Contract research

Many oil companies operate an extensive research and development programme, with well-equipped facilities and highly qualified people. The research and development programme is usually split into two parts – fundamental research into new technologies or new materials and applications research aimed at improving product performance.

To give even greater technical support to their customers and to improve the quality of their customer relations, oil companies provide contract research to customers who do not have the same level of research and development facilities.

IDENTIFY YOUR RESEARCH SKILLS

Begin by categorising the type of research projects which demonstrate your ability and your commitment to innovative solutions. This provides a basis for identifying new business opportunities and promoting the service.

GET TO KNOW YOUR CUSTOMER'S BUSINESS

By running presentations and seminars for key technical people in client companies, you can get to know the potential for contract research and you can demonstrate how you can add value to the customer's business. If you maintain service records, analyse recurring service problems to identify research opportunities.

INVOLVE THE CUSTOMER'S TECHNICAL TEAM

Invite members of your customer's technical team to submit their own ideas for research projects and evaluate their feasibility. Your research team should develop detailed proposals which show how the research would benefit the customer and how the customer's own staff can contribute to the project. Customer staff get the opportunity to improve their own skills and career opportunities by working alongside specialists in project teams. The customer benefits not only from specialist research, but also from skilled staff who can make a greater contribution to the business.

ACTION

- ▶ Could your customers make use of your research and development facilities?
- ▶ Do you have the capacity to handle additional research and development work?
- ▶ How relevant is your research and development work to that of your customers?
- ▶ Can you involve your customers in relevant research and development projects?

Providing technical support to your customers

When your product is essential to the reliable operation of your customers' products, you have the opportunity to build loyalty through technical support.

Lubrication, for example, is a key feature of most equipment maintenance programmes and proper lubrication schedules are essential to the cost-effective operation of the equipment.

Equipment manufacturers therefore rely heavily on oil companies for advice and guidance on the correct lubrication programme. This gives the oil company the opportunity to develop effective relations with the equipment manufacturer and to have their oil specified as the recommended lubricant for the whole life of the machine.

105

SPECIFYING THE SUPPORT PROGRAMME

A technical support programme might include:

- development of special lubricants for difficult operating conditions;
- designing components to make the most effective use of lubrication;
- conducting analysis of failed components to improve future designs;
- providing a field technical support team to work with equipment operators on site; and
- providing back up to distributors who do not have the necessary expertise.

PROVIDING TECHNICAL INFORMATION

To help engineers gain a better understanding of lubrication, the company produces an information video and a series of handbooks which help them plan their own lubrication requirements. The video and handbooks stress the benefits of working closely with the oil company's technical departments to get the best possible solution. Engineers are also offered a series of technical papers written by oil company experts which deal with specific technical problems or explain new developments in lubrication technology.

BUILDING TECHNICAL PARTNERSHIP

To build even closer links, customers' engineering staff are invited to become members of a technical partners club. They get special discounts on industry seminars where the oil company is participating, special offers on technical books and a monthly bulletin on the latest in lubrication technology.

ACTION

- ▶ **Do your customers rely on your technical expertise to support their own operations?**
- ▶ **Are customers aware of all the technical support services you can offer?**
- ▶ **Can you utilise your technical expertise to develop industry leadership?**
- ▶ **Can you tailor your technical service to the needs of special customers?**

Offering customers your core skills

Many oil companies have more than just products to sell; they have skills and resources which many other companies would like to be able to utilise. These 'core skills' can be sold to customers to help them set up or manage processes that are crucial to their own success.

SUPPORTING CUSTOMERS IN YOUR OWN MARKET

Oil producers, for example, provide consultancy and project management skills to customers who are commissioning new processing plant. Services like this are sometimes offered as an integral part of a package deal, but they can also be used to generate additional revenue and profit.

TRANSFERRING SKILLS TO OTHER MARKETS

The oil company identifies its core skills as designing and engineering complex processes. Although the company's expertise is related to the production of oil, the skills can be transferred to other industries.

ACTION

▶ **Do you have core skills which your customers could utilise?**

▶ **Can these core skills be sold to companies outside your traditional markets?**

▶ **What type of transferred experience can you offer prospects in the new market?**

107

▶ **Do your company's key strengths relate to important buying factors in other markets?**

Helping your customers manage their operations

Fleet petrol management is another example of the way oil companies can build loyalty by helping their customers manage costs efficiently.

Fleet fuel represents a major market for oil companies. Although petrol is a commodity item and there is not a significant variation in its price, fleet managers still need support in controlling their fuel costs.

The cost of financing fuel purchases can be a significant cost factor. Fleet managers need:

■ confirmation that expenditure classified as petrol is actually being spent on petrol;

■ the level of fuel consumption for each of their vehicles;

- an accurate indication of their present and future fuel costs; and

- advice on the best method of paying for their petrol – should they be using cash, credit card, accounts or should they pay petty cash on demand.

BASIC PAYMENT CARDS

A number of petrol companies have introduced fuel cards which allow named drivers to charge petrol costs and related motoring costs to their company in the same way as a credit card. However, these cards can be abused unless there are restrictions on the type of expenditure and they do not encourage loyalty to a brand of petrol unless they are restricted to certain types of service station.

A MORE FLEXIBLE CARD

The petrol company analyses the market for charge cards and spots a gap in the market. It surveys the needs of fleet operators and drivers to see the key buying patterns.

- Drivers want convenience and flexibility – not necessarily being tied to one petrol company – but being free to get petrol easily wherever they travel.

- Fleet operators want control over expenditure and high levels of management information so that they can manage their fuel costs individually.

The card they develop has all these features. Although it carries the company's identity, it can be used at any petrol station, giving the drivers the flexibility they need and reducing the fleet operators' dependency on a single petrol company.

LAUNCHING THE CARD TO RETAILERS

In their launch to their own retailers they stress that, although the card is not exclusive to any retail group, they represent the largest number of stations in the network and the high take-up of the card will give them a significant increase in business.

INFORMATION FOR FLEET OPERATORS

It is the level of management information which provides fleet operators with the greatest benefit and helps to build long-term relationships. The card is the basis of a sophisticated reporting system that gives the operator comprehensive information on total costs, costs per vehicle, vehicle performance and total fleet costs over different periods of time. A simple administrative system at the point of sale means that retailers can provide the management information without extra work – they simply ask the driver for current milage and the rest of the information comes from the card.

TAILORING A CARD SOLUTION FOR INDIVIDUAL FLEETS

The petrol company strengthens the relationship by developing tailored solutions for individual fleet operators which reflect their specific needs. For example, they can provide computerised information on line or they can integrate the petrol management information into their customers' own computers and reporting systems. They can also provide specialist staff on short-term assignment to the customer to establish and manage new information and control systems.

ENHANCING THE VALUE OF THE CARD

Some petrol companies have extended the card even further and put together a package which allows fleet drivers to charge for service and repairs as well as fuel. They negotiate agreements with car manufacturers' dealer networks to handle local service of fleet vehicles. Drivers pay for the service with their charge cards and the costs can be controlled through the same mechanism. They negotiate similar agreements with vehicle rescue organisations and suppliers of products like tyres and exhausts to increase convenience for the drivers. The package approach and the integrated management systems help to build the vital long-term loyalty with the major fleet operators.

ACTION

► **Can you provide management information and administrative services to support your customers' business processes?**

► **Have you got a realistic information infrastructure?**

Summary

Oil is a commodity product which competes with other forms of energy such as gas and electricity. The oil companies also compete with each other to secure long-term contracts and they use the quality of service to differentiate their offer. This service is based on helping their customers get the best from oil products and includes the following activities:

- providing contract research to customers as a means of getting involved in the customers' future plans and improving relationships;

- providing technical support to customers so that they rely on your technical expertise;

- offering customers your core skills to help them set up or manage activities that are crucial to their own success; and

- helping your customers manage their operations by providing them with access to your operating information and management skills.

These activities show the importance of helping your customers manage their own operations efficiently and offering skills which may be valuable to your customers' business.

11

Components suppliers

Components suppliers do not have a complete product to sell; their customers use their products to manufacture other products and their component may be only one small and relatively unimportant part of the final product. The components market is fragmented with many suppliers competing on price alone and with little opportunity for product differentiation.

Providing service support to your customers

When a company supplies components or replacement parts, it assumes that the buyer has the skills and resources to fit the components and maintain the equipment in the right condition. But, there is an opportunity to build a stronger relationship with customers by providing a level of service back-up that enables them to make the best use of their equipment. This support can take a number of forms:

- advice on setting up an efficient service operation;
- technical advice for customers who have the right support skills;
- training and technical manuals for customers who operate their own service department; and;
- contract service for customers who don't have a service department, but depend on efficient service for product reliability.

Service support programmes build customer loyalty by helping customers make the most effective use of the components they are buying.

Take a company which supplies parts to the construction equipment market. They are part of a group which makes construction equipment but they operate as an independent profit centre to concentrate on building a successful long-term business. They have a captive market in the first two years because warranty requires the equipment to be fitted with genuine manufacturer's parts. But, from the third year, the equipment owners have free choice and they buy spare parts on price and availability.

The company's competitors include:

- other equipment manufacturers who provide a range of fast moving products such as spark plugs, filters, or brake shoes, suitable for many different makes of equipment;

112

- specialist rebuilders who concentrate on high value components like axles, gearboxes or engines – they rebuild or refurbish older engines and sell replacements; and

- budget component suppliers who compete on the most popular parts and also provide low price and sometimes low quality replacements for larger components.

Most of the company's competitors concentrate on fast-moving components because they offer good volume business and the high level of repeat business is essential to customer loyalty. Speed of delivery and convenience are the main buying factors in this sector.

INCREASING CONVENIENCE

To improve convenience for equipment owners, the company sets up a series of regional fitting centres which provide an instant service on a range of popular repairs. Distributors provide the premises and the staff and the company manages and markets the programme. They issue promotional material to let equipment owners know about the service and they set up operating and training procedures to guarantee owners a quality rapid service. Distributors are highly motivated to provide the fitting service because it provides valuable revenue. They also offer a site fitting service for emergency breakdowns and more convenient servicing.

PROVIDING A QUALITY EXCHANGE SERVICE

To combat the engine rebuilders, the company sets up a network of exchange parts centres where construction equipment contractors can buy guaranteed factory-rebuilt components which are fitted by company-trained engineers. This helps to build customer loyalty by improving both quality and convenience.

INCREASING SERVICE COVERAGE

To provide national coverage, the company works with independent fitters. Fitters are a crucial factor in the market because they provide regular service and maintenance to a contractor's site. By building their loyalty, the company encourages them to specify their parts. They work closely with them to provide high levels of training and technical support, offer preferential discounts on parts sales and issue regular service bulletins so that the fitters always have the latest service information.

SUPPORTING CUSTOMERS' OWN WORKSHOPS

By supporting customers' workshops, they can combat the threat from competitive parts. They offer them an initial discount which is volume-related plus a complete package of support which is designed to lock the customers in. They provide the initial advice and guidance and training needed to establish an efficient workshop operation, including training for the technicians and advice on how to set up and manage a parts warehouse. The company holds emergency stocks of an itemised stock list and they provide technical documentation to help the service staff. These services are provided free of charge and help customers to run an efficient cost-effective service operation. Support like this helps to build valuable long-term relationships.

E

PROVIDING MANAGEMENT INFORMATION

To build the loyalty of larger parts users the company installed a computerised service database and online ordering system which provided their service staff with comprehensive technical information and diagnostic material. Service staff could use the information to diagnose problems quickly and identify the parts they need. The service became an integral part of the customer's operations and helped to improve the efficiency of his or her own operations.

All the above activities helped the company to increase its share of the market and made it difficult for competitors to recapture share or enter the market.

ACTION

114

► **Can you help your customers to run their own service operations?**

► **Can you identify independent service operations which help you provide a better service to your customers?**

► **Can you use management information to support your customers' operations?**

Branding a commodity product

Replacement parts are a form of distress purchase and buyers are generally concerned with price and availability, rather than quality and performance. But to build customer loyalty over the long term, a component supplier needs to build awareness of the qualities of his product and ensure that it is his products that are specified. This can be achieved by branding the products and building brand awareness and loyalty.

Branding is widely used in consumer marketing but it is less common in business-to-business products. The theory behind branding is that a product requires a 'personality' which customers instantly recognise. The 'brand values' describe the features and benefits that have the highest customer appeal and they are communicated regularly to the target market.

IDENTIFYING BRAND VALUES

The most important brand values for a component manufacturer are quality and reliability, but they are not the only factors that influence buyers – value for money, technical back up, availability and service support are also seen as important. Information like this enables a component supplier to build up a brand profile for their product and forms the basis for design and communications programmes.

CHOOSING A BRAND NAME

The starting point for the programme is a brand name which applies to all products. A fictitious example is 'OMNIA' which suggests a wide product range, universal fitting and quality. The name can be applied to every product and also to the dealers who sell the products. The name was also applied to support services and systems, and this helped to build brand strength by demonstrating that the company could offer customers a complete service rather than just a product - a factor which helped to differentiate the company from the competition.

DEVELOPING A BRAND IDENTITY

The brand name is reinforced by a strong design identity which is applied to all visual elements. A logo is the focal point for this identity, together with special colours and a corporate typeface. The combination of these three elements gives the brand a number of qualities – it is immediately recognisable, easily distinguished from its competitors and memorable. The identity is applied to product packaging, display and all communications material so that there is a consistent and strong brand identity.

CONTROLLING THE BRAND IDENTITY

Controlling the brand identity is an essential task, particularly when promotional material is not produced centrally. Variations in the treatment can dilute the strength of a brand identity so strict guidelines are needed to ensure that standards are maintained. It is equally important that the company communicates consistent messages about its products and brand values.

MATCHING SERVICE TO THE BRAND IMAGE

The test of a brand image is the customer's perception so it is important that customers receive a consistently high standard of service and that products are of the highest quality. Branding alone is not sufficient to build sales and long-term repeat business – the brand promise has to be backed by the right qualities.

116

Branding can help companies differentiate their products in a commodity market and make it easier to introduce new products or sell additional products from the range.

ACTION

► **Can you identify the brand values that will make your products stand out in the marketplace?**

► **Can you control the way brand values are used?**

► **Can you transfer brand values to other products in your range?**

Providing customers with their own range of branded components

A number of component suppliers provide replacement parts to equipment manufacturers who hold stocks to support their own repair and service operations. The equipment manufacturers depend on a quality service to maintain their competitive edge and continuity of supply to their customers.

However, they require a wide range of components from a variety of specialist suppliers to provide a complete service to their customers. Quality varies between suppliers so the equipment manufacturer is unable to offer a consistent supply. One supplier recommends an 'own label' range of replacement parts which would carry the equipment manufacturers' brand name and conform to the manufacturer's own quality standards.

MANAGING THE PROGRAMME FOR CUSTOMERS

The component supplier manages the programme for the customer, supplying their own products to an agreed specification and quality standard, and managing the procurement and distribution of other suppliers' products. This ensures that all the products are produced to the same standards and delivery can be controlled to minimise the customer's stock holding costs. The equipment supplier does not have to invest his own resources or train staff in new skills. The equipment supplier is also able to deliver a higher standard of service to his own customers.

117

BRANDING THE CUSTOMERS' PRODUCTS

The components supplier takes this partnership by helping the equipment supplier set up an own label operation supplying replacement parts for other manufacturers' equipment – an all-makes operation. The branded parts are distributed through the equipment manufacturer's authorised dealer network and through a number of independent retail outlets who buy from OEM as a wholesaler. The customer is able to draw on the supplier's retail experience to package the branded parts and develop a retail support strategy that enables them to build strong market share.

Although the range competes indirectly with the component supplier's own products, it increases demand for the supplier's products and improves the business relationship.

ACTION

► **Could your customers improve their business performance by offering a range of components under their own brand name?**

► **Can you help your customers improve their service to their own customers?**

► **Can you manage some of the activities that will enable your customers to compete effectively?**

Helping your customers reduce their costs

Working on a joint design project with your customers is an effective way of building partnership. When a component supplier becomes part of the customer design team, he or she builds a dependent relationship that goes beyond mere technical advice and guidance.

118

Value engineering is one of the ways in which this can be explained; it is a design technique which helps engineers reduce the cost of a product through design and helps them achieve further economies through simplified assembly or reduced maintenance costs. Manufacturers who use the service can offer higher performance, greater reliability or lower prices to their ultimate customer. The component supplier is helping the customer achieve a cost-effective solution.

This is an example of the process. A bearing supplier worked closely with the designer of a piece of agricultural equipment to analyse the number of components needed to support and maintain the bearing. They reduced a complex assembly from six components to one by developing a complete unit which contained the bearing, its housing, a lubrication channel and a protective cover. The manufacturer simply bolted the single component in position. The benefits were significant:

■ assembly time was reduced;

■ the number of components was reduced, saving manufacturing time and costs; and

■ reliability was improved and maintenance reduced.

As a result of that project, the component supplier won an increased level of orders and improved relationships with the customer. The customer recognised the contribution the service was making and reviewed opportunities to use value engineering on other products in the range.

USING VALUE ENGINEERING TO COMBAT PRICE COMPETITION

Component suppliers can use value engineering to build effective relationships with customers by offering them real value for money. They can also give themselves a competitive advantage when they are faced with price competition. By helping customers to reduce overall 'through life' costs, suppliers build a dependent relationship.

119

ESTABLISHING THE RIGHT CONTACTS

Suppliers need to get close to their customer so that they can get involved at the design stage of a project, not when the specification is complete and the order is being placed. The important contacts are the designers and the technical staff, not just the purchasing staff who place the orders.

BUILDING A NEW BUSINESS PROJECT TEAM

The first stage in the process was to train the sales force to adopt this new approach to business development. They give the sales force guidelines on identifying the important contacts and they run seminars to explain how value engineering operates. By encouraging the sales force to work closely with the engineering department, they were able to build an effective new business team.

EDUCATING THE MARKET

The company used direct marketing and editorial to communicate the benefits of this new service to customers. Feature articles in the design engineering press explained the approach to design through a series of case histories.

Copies of the case histories were mailed to key contacts with an invitation to a seminar or a presentation on the customer's premises. The case histories helped to build the company's credibility while the presentations provide an opportunity to find out about their customer's current design projects and to make initial recommendations.

ACTION

▶ **Can you use your technical skills to improve your customers' design process?**

▶ **Are you aware of your customers' design plans?**

▶ **Can you transfer cost reduction processes to other sections of the market?**

Building confidence through quality

When customers know you have a reputation for quality, they will rely on your products for consistently high standards of performance.

Component suppliers can register under their industry quality schemes as approved suppliers. This demonstrates that they have achieved exacting standards in the production and quality control of their products and this builds customer confidence.

Quality is a key differentiator and one that your company should exploit.

TELL CUSTOMERS ABOUT QUALITY

Advertising and promotional material should carry a symbol of any appropriate quality standards you have achieved and you should explain the tangible benefits of quality for your customers.

AIM TO ACHIEVE INDUSTRY LEADERSHIP IN QUALITY

One component supplier decided to increase the length of its warranty so that they could offer the best terms in the industry. That gave them an immediate strategic advantage because it positioned them as a company committed to quality.

USE EXTENDED GUARANTEES TO BUILD SERVICE LOYALTY

They then offered an extended guarantee on all components that were fitted and serviced by an authorised dealer. The guarantee went beyond the normal period and gave their customers additional peace of mind. The programme was also useful in building dealer loyalty – it gave dealers additional parts and service revenue and made them the first choice for parts.

121

HELPING YOUR CUSTOMERS ACHIEVE QUALITY

The company offered free quality seminars to customer staff. These seminars explained to customers how they could apply the same quality principles to their products and how supplier and customer could work in partnership to improve overall quality.

ACTION

► **How important is quality to your customers?**

► **Can you convert quality promises to tangible benefits such as improved warranties?**

► **Do your customers understand why quality is an important buying factor?**

Improving delivery times

In the market for replacement parts, one of the key buying factors is speed of delivery. One strategy for improving market share is to concentrate on developing a rapid response to customer requests. It is not essential in every sector because other factors such as quality of support or technical competence rate higher, but it is possible to identify a number of sectors where speed of response could win a contract or maintain the loyalty of a customer.

In the construction equipment market, for example, contractors have to keep their equipment in action. An idle machine not only costs money but slows down progress on a contract.

TAILORING A SERVICE

The components supplier negotiated a series of replacement parts contracts with their major construction customers. The supplier would be the major supplier of parts for a two-year period and, in return, they agreed to hold reserve stocks of a number of parts which were critical to continued operation. When the contractor needed the parts they would be delivered within a pre-determined time. A site fitting service and emergency cover were also included in the package. Pre-planned deliveries were scheduled on computer and could be modified through experience to meet seasonal requirements.

IMPROVING THE DELIVERY SERVICE

To maintain and improve the high level of response it was essential to involve wholesalers and independent distributors. The component supplier worked closely with them to ensure they provided the right level of service. They produced a programme guide which explained how to manage a stockholding system and they provided distributors with information on customer purchasing patterns.

ACTION

► **Can you identify customers with a requirement for rapid service response?**

► **Are you set up to respond to emergency requests?**

▶ **Can you use distributors to reduce stockholding levels, while still maintaining a responsive service?**

Using technical consultancy to build partnership

Traditionally, customers have forced component suppliers to treat price as the most important sales factor, and that does little to build customer loyalty. But, when a supplier can provide customers with a technical service that helps them to improve the performance of their own business, that can form the basis of a valuable relationship. The customer's dependence on the technical support can often overcome price problems and give the supplier a competitive edge.

IMPROVING CUSTOMERS' TECHNICAL PERFORMANCE

123

A supplier produces industrial sealants for a wide range of applications. Their customers include manufacturers in high-technology industries like aerospace, where applications are extremely demanding. The supplier uses his technological edge to develop partnerships with a number of key customers. The supplier became deeply involved in development projects and was able to develop a number of patented components which put them in the forefront of the industry.

BUILDING TECHNICAL PARTNERSHIP

A series of presentations and seminars for design directors was used to establish the supplier as a technically advanced company with the research and development facilities to handle complex and advanced development projects. It covered the company's track record in innovation and showed how it had worked in partnership with other customers. At the presentation, the company took the opportunity to introduce members of the technical team and to explain its approach to development programmes. The aim was to build confidence in the customer's technical department. To maintain the relationship, the supplier published quarterly technical updates which provided information on current research projects.

SELLING THE MARKETING BENEFITS OF TECHNOLOGY

The suppliers claimed that a technologically advanced component would improve the performance or cost-effectiveness of the customer's products. This would help the customer improve the quality of its own products and add to its own competitive edge. By working closely with the customer's marketing department the supplier was able to strengthen the partnership.

ACTION

▶ **Do your customers depend on your technical services to support their own business?**

▶ **Are your customers trying to improve their own technical performance?**

▶ **Can you supplement your customers' resources with your own research facilities?**

▶ **Are customers aware of your technical facilities and record of innovation?**

Improving nationwide service by helping distributors build local businesses

Too many components suppliers rely on their distributors for turnover and profit, but don't do much to support them. 'It's their business, they're responsible for running it and, if they don't perform, we can always appoint another dealer.' That means distributors get token support including standard advertisements and mailers which might not be relevant to their own business.

But the dealer is actually running a small independent business tuned to his local market. The proper way for the component supplier to behave is to invest in the success of that local business. Investment does not mean just money – although a stake in the business demonstrates a real commitment to partnership – it includes:

- training to develop the skills of the dealership;
- systems so that both parties can share information; and
- local marketing support at the wholesale and retail level.

Many companies have tried to impose their national marketing policy on distributors without taking account of the distributors' real strengths which include an understanding of the local market. National advertising and promotional campaigns are used to attract prospects into the dealership. Once there, they argue, it is the dealer's responsibility to convert them to customers.

125

IMPROVING STAFF SKILLS

Although advertising and promotion can generate a high level of enquiries, conversion demands other skills. Distributor sales staff behind the counter or on the road tend to be young – newcomers to the business – with only a small amount of product knowledge. More experienced members of staff are promoted to management positions and have little direct contact with customers. This can be frustrating for customers – they want advice and guidance and technical back-up but the staff are not capable of delivering it. Training in sales skills and product knowledge is essential but the training must be related to local business conditions. Training delivered on the distributor's premises can be tailored to match the individual skills profile and business objectives.

RETAINING CUSTOMERS

Training enables the distributor to deliver a higher standard of customer service and this helps to build repeat business – customers feel they are dealing with a professional. When they want advice and guidance, the professional dealership is first choice.

DEVELOPING A LOCAL BUSINESS PLAN

The business plan was an important factor in building the relationship and increasing sales. The business plan was built on the dealer's understanding of local business conditions and was essentially a local marketing plan to which ABC committed resources and support. The company found that instead of increasing the administrative problems of managing its dealership support programme it actually simplified it because the tailoring and selection of programmes was handled at local level. ABC found that their support programme represented much better value for money because they were producing targeted results.

Summary

The components market is highly fragmented with fierce price competition and little opportunity for product differentiation. The strategies include:

- providing service support to customers to improve their own skills and provide a better overall service;
- branding commodity products to differentiate them from the competition;
- providing customers with their own range of branded components so that they can provide a quality service to their own ultimate customers;
- helping your customers reduce costs by working in partnership with their design team;
- building confidence through quality;
- improving delivery times to demonstrate customer care;
- using technical consultancy to build partnership; and
- providing customers with an efficient local service by supporting distributors.

Like the oil companies, components manufacturers can use service and management skills to strengthen customer relationships and reduce the impact of price competition.

12

Travel agent programmes

Improving standards of customer service

Travel agents are a vital link between travel companies and consumers. They provide essential information, take bookings and help customers plan their holidays. To deliver the right standard of service they depend on the quality of their own staff and the information provided to them by the travel companies. Their income is determined by the commission they gain from the sale of holiday and associated services.

HELPING INDEPENDENTS TO SET HIGH STANDARDS

Larger groups of travel agents have well-established training programmes and a high level of central support for their business. The independent travel agents offer a higher level of flexibility but do not enjoy the same levels of business support. A consortium of smaller travel companies decide to work with independent travel agents to help them develop their own business.

MEETING CUSTOMER REQUIREMENTS

Consumer research on attitudes to travel agents identify the key strengths of the independents which are flexibility, personal service and greater choice. Their perceived weaknesses are slow administration and more complicated booking procedures. Some consumers were not aware of the range of services available from independent travel agents.

IMPROVING BUSINESS PERFORMANCE

The consortium utilised a computer bureau service to set up a network of local computer facilities which were linked to a central enquiry and reservation system. This gave the independents the strength of central booking facilities and ensured that they could offer the same speed and quality of service as the larger groups. To improve business efficiency, the computer programmes incorporated an administrative package which handled accounts, bookings and other administrative tasks and gave staff more time for selling and customer contact.

MAKING CONSUMERS AWARE OF THE SERVICE

Part of the funding for the travel agents was used to run an advertising campaign locally and nationally to raise awareness of independent travel services. This stressed the personal service available from independents and explained how they were grouping together to make more effective use of central management and marketing resources.

The close co-operation between the independents helped them to compete effectively with larger rivals and provide the quality of service which retained customers.

ACTION

- ► **Can you improve the performance of retail outlets by providing them with business support?**
- ► **Do you have the facilities to provide centralised support or do you need to utilise third-party services?**

Improving the quality of travel information

When people are planning a journey – whether it's for business, holiday or personal reasons – they want to be able to get more than just tickets and schedules from a travel company. They need information on other destinations, they need to know what documents they need and they may need advice and guidance on local conditions if they are inexperienced travellers.

CENTRALISED INFORMATION SYSTEMS

A group of local independent travel agents pool their resources to set up a central information service which is available to all their members. This features a central reference library which contains or identifies sources of information on most popular destinations. The centre publishes a series of traveller's guides to help customers make their own arrangements and travel with greater confidence.

DEVELOPING A SPECIALIST TRAVEL SERVICE

129

To extend the range of services available to customers who want to make their own travel arrangements, rather than book a package through a travel agent, the centre builds information on self-catering holidays, car hire, hotels, domestic travel and other services that might be relevant. This allows holidaymakers to tailor their own holiday and to let customers know about this, the centre publishes a magazine which includes stories about people who have created their own holidays.

OFFERING A PERSONAL TRAVEL SERVICE

Staff at individual branches are trained in the skills of holiday development and are given full details of the central information service. By concentrating on the tailored approach the independent travel agents are able to offer a service better suited to their size and skills. They cannot match the national chains in purchasing power, so it is difficult for them to compete on the standard packaged programmes. But they can develop the edge on dealing with the more unusual travel requirements and the high level of personal service they are able to offer.

ACTION

- ▶ **Can you share resources to improve your competitive edge?**
- ▶ **Is there an advantage in competing on personal service rather than price?**
- ▶ **How can you personalise your service to improve customer service?**

Packaging services for the business traveller

A significant percentage of the travel industry's turnover is derived from business travel and it is essential that the marketing programme reflects this. Convenience and cost-effectiveness are the prime requirements in this sector. Business people need to know that there are regular connections between the most important business centres and that costs are competitive. They need to know that they will be able to travel in comfort with a reasonable level of service and they want to know that help and advice is available if it's needed. They need to be convinced that the carrier keeps to time so that their schedules will not be disrupted and that they can book travel services easily.

A coach operator decided to launch a coach service between British business centres and developed a package of services which positioned his coaches as a viable alternative to domestic airlines, railways and private/company cars.

ANALYSING RAILWAY COMPETITION

Trains, although they were fast and frequent, were subject to late arrivals, cancellations and overcrowding. Business travellers got over the problem of overcrowding by paying first-class fares, but this made the journey more expensive and they had no control over punctuality. Stations were located in the main business centres, but the business traveller had to get to these stations and make separate arrangements to get to his final destination.

ANALYSING AIRLINE COMPETITION

Airlines offer even shorter journey times and had a proven record of punctuality and availability, but they were less frequent, the destinations were fewer and the departure points were probably less convenient than stations. Travel costs were higher although the faster flight times gave more time for business and the traveller probably wouldn't need hotel accommodation, so the overall cost was comparative.

ANALYSING COMPETITION FROM CARS

Travelling by car offered the highest levels of convenience – the journey was door to door and journey time could be quick provided the roads were clear and the journey was not too long. Potentially, it was the cheapest form of transport if only petrol costs were taken into consideration, but this did not take into account the running costs of the car, additional wear and tear, parking costs, overnight accommodation, longer journeys – and driver stress.

DEVELOPING A COMPETITIVE SERVICE

The coach operator identified the car as the main competitor. Coaches could offer the same levels of frequency and reliability as an airline, and there was less stress on the traveller. They could offer the same journey time between major destinations as a car and, to improve convenience for drivers, they offered a free feeder or parking service as well as a free courtesy car which covered final destinations within a fifteen-mile radius of the main arrival points.

ADDING CONVENIENCE TO THE SERVICE

The service on the coaches was planned to suit the needs of the business traveller with reserved seating, meals on board, mobile phones and fax and computer facilities so that people could use the time to work or meet. Part of the coach was divided off as a private meeting room which could be booked in advance. The coach operator also made arrangements with hotels and car-hire companies in the area so that it was able to offer comprehensive booking facilities. To encourage loyalty, it offered special bonuses to frequent travellers and discounts for individual travellers and corporate buyers.

By analysing all the factors that influenced the business traveller, the coach company was able to develop a programme that had a wide appeal and would guarantee high levels of customer satisfaction and loyalty.

ACTION

- ► **Can you develop a package of services to appeal to a specific target audience?**
- ► **Have you developed a package that meets all competitive threats?**
- ► **Can your service be enhanced to add even greater value?**

132

Building the loyalty of travel agents with reservation systems

Up-to-date information is vital in the travel business. Manual booking and reservation systems were just too slow – the travel agent had to telephone to find out what seats or holidays were available, get a final decision from the customer and then confirm bookings. Issuing tickets, invoices and other documents added to the administrative burden. When several carriers or travel companies offered services to the same destination, then the travel agents' enquiry stage was even more complicated.

PROVIDING RAPID ACCESS TO INFORMATION

The major carriers tried to simplify this by installing computer links in travel agencies and issuing their information on computer. This led to accusations of bias – especially from the smaller carriers who were not able to offer similar facilities. When global reservation facilities were introduced this gave each carrier the opportunity to provide information on equal, unbiased terms.

The marketing initiative in travel information shifted from the carriers, who had used this as a method of controlling travel agents, to information providers who were usually subsidiary companies of major airlines. The information suppliers were able to provide the same level of information to small and large travel agents alike using different variations of personal computer. The overall benefit was to the consumer, but it gave travel agents and travel companies the opportunity to operate more efficiently.

HELPING TRAVEL AGENCIES IMPROVE THEIR BUSINESS

The information providers marketed their services to large and small travel agencies at a number of different levels. When they were talking to major multiples they made headquarters present-ations to the operating directors outlining the potential gains in competitive edge and business efficiency. They explained how a computerised system would simplify the administration and issu-ing system and increase customer satisfaction through a speedier, more efficient service. They showed how the individual branch systems could be linked together to provide greater headquarters control and information. They agreed to support the introduction of the system with project management, training and a back-up service to the branches.

133

They also provided a business builder package which was launched to headquarters and the branches. This built the com-mitment of branch staff because it showed how the branches could increase their business by using the new package. It would free staff from routine administration and allow them more oppor-tunity to concentrate on selling and customer follow up. When they were talking to smaller travel agents they pitched on the basis of this being an affordable system which would enable the independents to compete with the major chains.

MAINTAINING THE QUALITY OF THE SERVICE

The information providers also had to develop partnerships with the companies who issued travel information to ensure that its system was comprehensive. By adding other types of travel information such as hotel profiles, car hire rates and local facilities, they were able to increase the value of the system to travel agents and that ensured their long-term loyalty.

ACTION

▶ **Can you use information services to build the loyalty of your customers?**

▶ **How can you ensure that the information meets all their requirements?**

▶ **Can you add value to the information service?**

Demonstrating the quality of service

Customer service should be at the heart of a travel company's marketing programme, but to achieve high standards of customer service takes more than just an advertising campaign and superficial smiles. An airline draws up a customer service programme which it believes should reflect the real needs of its customers.

SURVEYING CUSTOMER NEEDS

The process begins with a survey to identify what these needs are and to identify the major business and training requirements. Two key points came out of the survey – customers want to arrive at their destinations and they want to be kept informed if there are likely to be delays.

RESPONDING TO THE SURVEY

Many factors affecting punctuality lie outside the airline's control but they identify the elements that they can control such as check-in procedures, turn-round times between flights and tighter controls over suppliers, service staff and subcontractors. They also improve their facilities for getting information to passengers – the indicator boards, the announcements and the management of the information. By appointing an information co-ordinator and setting standards for receiving and communicating information the company is able to improve its performance in this area.

IMPROVING CUSTOMER CARE

Customers also indicated that they wanted better standards of care. This extended from advice and guidance for the inexperienced traveller to detailed information about services at the destination. It also covered factors like courtesy at the check-in and the quality of in-flight service.

135

BUILDING COMMITMENT TO CUSTOMER CARE

To provide the right level of customer care, the company identifies key staff and sets up training programmes to help them achieve the right standards. It also introduces a customer care programme in which all staff have to participate. The programme describes the contribution every member of staff can make and shows how these improvements will help to build customer loyalty and ensure future jobs. The changes in customer satisfaction are measured over a period of time and groups and individuals who have made a significant improvement are rewarded.

DIVIDING CUSTOMER CARE INTO INDIVIDUAL ACTIONS

By identifying a series of specific actions which small groups can take within a defined time period, the company is able to manage and measure a series of individual tasks. Provided all the individual tasks fit within the strategic framework, this is likely to have a greater impact than a single strategic programme which looks for general improvement.

ACTION

▶ **How important is customer care to your customers?**

▶ **Can you translate customer care into a series of specific actions that can be easily managed?**

▶ **Are your staff committed to customer care?**

Maintaining contact with travel customers

Regular contact with the customer is one way of building long-term relationships, and travel companies have an opportunity to build up valuable traveller profiles which can form the basis of effective direct marketing programmes.

BUILDING A DATABASE

Business travellers can be categorised by frequency of travel, destination and starting points, annual expenditure, additional services, methods of payment, type of business and other factors.

Although holidaymakers travel less frequently, it is possible to build up simpler profiles which identify levels of expenditure, destinations, methods of payment and additional services.

BUILDING A RELATIONSHIP WITH TRAVELLERS

Direct marketing can build contact between journeys, make customers aware of additional or new services and build loyalty by making them feel part of a club. It can also help travel agents and carriers make more effective use of their communications budget by improving targeting or by complementing other communications programmes.

DEVELOPING SPECIFIC NEW BUSINESS THROUGH DIRECT MARKETING

A domestic airline which operated from a number of regional

centres wants to expand its business from these centres. It uses national and regional advertising to make consumers aware of its service and routes. But its direct marketing focuses on the types of business people most likely to fly between these destinations. The information for this comes from an analysis of existing customers and the types of business found in both regions. In marketing to Scottish companies, for example, the company finds a close match between oil, chemical, finance and civil engineering companies in Scotland and London. It develops a mailing list which it uses to contact these high-profile sectors with details of its services and any new offers as they happen. This helps to raise awareness, make specific offers and also provides a useful channel for launching new products. Every customer gets information on new services or changes to existing services and arrangements. When it introduces new European routes, it uses the same principles of targeting key business sectors and using direct mail to inform them of the new routes and of any reciprocal travel arrangements available.

137

BUILDING THE LOYALTY OF EXISTING CUSTOMERS

The company also uses direct marketing to maintain contact with its existing customers. It has a pre-established programme to offer loyalty bonuses or special offers to frequent travellers. For example, it offers special car hire rates and the facilities of a gold club to people who travel more than five times a year. This gives the frequent traveller a sense of belonging and specific privileges.

ACTION

► **Have you got a comprehensive profile of your customer base?**
► **Are you using this information to maintain contact with your customers?**
► **Can you use targeted mailing to attack specific markets?**

Summary

Success in the travel industry, like many other businesses depends on understanding customers' needs and developing the skills and products to meet those needs. The key management activities include:

- improving standards of customer service in retail outlets;
- improving the quality of customer information to enhance high standards of personal service;
- packaging services for specific market sectors so that they reflect customers' real needs;
- building the loyalty of distributors by supporting their business operations;
- demonstrating the quality of service by operating a highly visible customer care programme; and
- maintaining contact with customers through planned direct marketing programmes.

These principles can be applied to any service business where the quality of people is important.

13

Delivering consultancy services

Increasing contact through complete business solutions

Consultancy, like many other services, is delivered as a series of ad hoc projects. When the project is completed, there is no guaranteed continuity of relationship. Yet the consultancy needs to be aware of the customer's changing business requirements if it is to deliver appropriate advice and guidance, and the customer will benefit from regular, informed consultancy to maintain the impetus of its business initiatives. Although many consultancies enjoy a high level of repeat business, this is not the same as a long-term relationship, so it is important to build the confidence of customers and convince them that they will benefit from continued consultancy.

USING THE LIFE CYCLE TO IDENTIFY OPPORTUNITIES

The total business solution is one method of building continuity of contact. Here, a consultancy takes total responsibility for the implementation of a project and continues to be involved over the life of a project. The life-cycle concept, explained in Chapter 3, describes how customers' needs change over time. Increasingly, consultancies are offering implementation, project management, training and other services to support their customers' business activities. Although the consultancy may not provide these services itself, it needs to understand them and manage them, if necessary. In this way, the customer is sure of continued support at every stage, while the consultancy enjoys continuity of work.

EXPLAINING THE IMPORTANCE OF BUSINESS SOLUTIONS

It is important to brief the customers on the benefits of this closer relationship. In the past, the consultancy has published a services brochure which simply lists and describes the individual services it offers; however, this brochure does not help customers understand the strategic importance of services or the long-term benefits of working together. A new introductory brochure explains, through case histories, the concept of the life cycle and shows how the customer's needs change at every stage.

To build understanding of the total business solution, the consultancy runs a series of seminars using actual business scenarios from the company's own business. The scenarios identify the customer's requirements and show how the consultancy can provide services to meet those requirements.

PRESENTING CAPABILITY

The consultancy also has to prove that it has the skills and resources to deliver or manage the complete solution. Research shows customers understand the traditional skills of management consultancy, but need reassurance about the consultancy's capability in training, implementation, project management, maintenance and other services. It uses the management press to communicate its new approach to business and to explain individual services. Interviews with senior executives of customers who have implemented the total solution help to give credibility to the consultancy's case.

ACTION

- ► **Does your business have a pattern of ad hoc projects?**
- ► **Can you introduce other services to support your core business?**

▶ **Do your customers need specific services to make the most of your core services?**

▶ **Do customers understand the benefits of a total solution?**

▶ **Do customers understand your capability in this area?**

Improving customers' management skills

Consultancies sometimes take their customers into unfamiliar territory where they have little experience and where they feel they are unable to make effective management decisions. This means that management teams may be cautious about implementing new strategies because they are unsure of the consequences and that caution may lead to consultancy recommendations being rejected or postponed.

141

One way to tackle this is through executive briefings which explain the fundamentals and benefits of the new proposals. These can take the form of published guides which give general background on a business issue, or they can be presentations which deal with individual customer concerns.

IDENTIFYING OPPORTUNITIES

A consultancy specialising in manufacturing development has helped customers implement a number of computer-based manufacturing solutions, and they are in the forefront of consultancy for the Just-In-Time (JIT) approach to manufacturing. Government surveys of manufacturing industry reveal a fundamental lack of understanding of the requirements of JIT which calls for a high level of computerisation, but also needs a complete reappraisal of the way a factory is managed. For the JIT initiative to succeed, the consultants will need to be involved much more deeply in their customers' day-to-day business. The consultants work closely with an industry association to develop management guidelines on the introduction of JIT.

RAISING AWARENESS OF THE NEED FOR CHANGE

The first stage is a series of senior management seminars held at the consultancy's executive briefing centre – a prestige building with facilities for presentation and discussion. Senior executives participate in presentations and seminars which take them through the key decision making stages. The seminars ensure that the consultancy's work is discussed at the right level and that key executives understand the issues they face.

HELPING CUSTOMERS IMPLEMENT CHANGE

The consultancy backs up the seminars with working documents explaining how customers can implement the consultancy recommendations. The documents help senior executives to turn their recommendations into action. The consultancy briefs the executives on all the implications of the changes so they will not overestimate the results they are likely to achieve. It would be easy for a customer to believe that consultancy can solve all business problems, but the customer should be aware of the responsibilities and actions they must take to ensure success.

BUILDING CONFIDENCE IN CUSTOMERS

The executive briefing is an important stage in building long-term relationships. It builds confidence in customers, makes them receptive to the consultancy recommendations, ensures that they understand the full implications of a programme and builds a professional relationship.

ACTION

- ▶ Do your customers have skills to implement your recommendations successfully?
- ▶ Do customers understand the management implications of your consultancy recommendations?
- ▶ Are you making your customers aware of the strategic importance of change?
- ▶ Do you give practical guidelines on the implementation of change?

142

Working with your customer's management team

For a consultancy to succeed in the long term, it is important that its customers are committed to the programme at the highest level. If the customer is sympathetic, this can lead to effective results, but if the customer has no real understanding of the major issues, or the professional skills to implement recommendations effectively, the benefits to both customer and consultancy could be short-lived.

SHORT-TERM STAFF ASSIGNMENTS

Design management, for example, helps companies get the best possible results from a design project without recruiting specialist staff. Here a senior partner from a design consultancy works on a long- or short-term assignment for the company at senior level to ensure that the decision-making process and the implementation of the project are effective. If a company is undertaking a redesign of its complete range of products, a large number of people in the company will be involved, and good results will depend on effective co-ordination.

143

WORKING AT THE RIGHT LEVEL

Detailed design decisions will be taking place on a day-to-day basis, but there will also be high-level strategy decisions to be made regularly, so the consultant must be able to work at both levels. The detailed involvement ensures that the consultancy gets all the information and support it needs and that the key people are available when needed.

The customer benefits because he gets a continued level of objective advice from an experienced professional without having to recruit or retrain his own staff to meet short-term requirements.

ACTION

► **Do your customers need regular support for their management team?**

▶ **Do you have the skills to provide direct support to your customers?**

▶ **Are you working at the right level?**

Developing your customers' staff

Successful consultancy provides an effective business solution that should make the customer more competitive and able to meet his strategic objectives. But the long-term effectiveness of the consultancy depends on how well the customer can implement the solution and maintain the impetus. If the customers' staff do not have the skills or the understanding, the advice may not be effectively implemented and the customer may not believe that the consultancy is a success. When it comes to placing the next project it may not automatically go to the consultancy.

IDENTIFYING KEY STAFF

To ensure this long-term relationship and provide the customer with added value, the consultancy introduces a staff development service. They identify the staff who are crucial to the success of a project and plan long- and short-term staff development programmes. Training is an integral part of any consultancy project but this is normally concentrated on the users. However, it is the managers and supervisory staff who may be the weak links. They need to know when to take action, when to make changes and how to measure the performance of their staff. The consultancy also needs to ensure that executives are committed to the long-term success of the project and that they will continue to invest and provide the right level of resources to carry it out properly. The staff development programme is crucial, not only to the customer's success, but to the long-term success of the consultancy.

BUILDING THE COMMITMENT OF CUSTOMER STAFF

To introduce the training programme, the consultancy develops a presentation which focuses on the factors behind effective implementation and analyses the customer's staff development requirements. The client can then see the problems and opportunities and is closely involved in the programme development. To help the customer communicate the benefits of the development programme, the consultancy develops an internal communications programme which explains how each member of the staff can make a personal contribution to the success of the business and outlines the type of training that will help them to achieve it.

ACTION

► **How critical are staff skills to the success of your project?**

► **Can you identify the people who influence the success of a project?**

► **Can you help your customer build the commitment of their staff?**

145

Extending consultancy into implementation and maintenance

Management consultancies working in Information Technology (IT) have traditionally provided high level strategic consultancy on the right IT solutions, but they have been losing revenue to systems manufacturers and independent software vendors who are providing their own consultancy to build customer loyalty and increase revenue and profit.

BROADENING THE SERVICE BASE

The management consultancies see an opportunity to build their turnover and profit and to maintain control of their IT consultancy business by broadening the base of their services. They recognise from the life-cycle analysis that a large and increasing proportion of IT expenditure is going on implementation and

F

maintenance, and that these are regarded by customers as key activities.

DEVELOPING NEW SKILLS

To deliver implementation and maintenance, the consultancy has to develop a range of new skills and resources so that it can offer customers a service that is better than competitive offerings. The consultancy builds up its skills by hiring a small number of experienced project managers and building up a working partnership with specialist suppliers who can work to the standards required. Recruitment advertisements and literature explain the changing nature of the consultancy and show how this will introduce new career opportunities.

BUILDING PARTNERSHIP WITH SUPPLIERS

The consultancy develops presentations to explain to potential service partners how they will improve their own business opportunities. The presentation also lays down the standards of service that the consultancy requires from its partners and shows how the standards will be controlled. The consultancy acts as a facilities manager, delivering the service to an agreed quality standard.

WORKING WITH THE CUSTOMER'S MANAGEMENT TEAM

The customer needs reassurance that he will benefit by changing his traditional supplier to get the best possible solution. The consultancy explains the strategic importance of integrating IT services. It also demonstrates the savings in 'through life' costs which can be achieved with an integrated service. The consultancy reviews the detailed implementation with the management team responsible for support, showing the full range of skills available and demonstrating how its involvement as a facilities manager will help to improve the effectiveness of the support operation by freeing the customer team for more strategic tasks.

The move into implementation and maintenance helps the consultancy expand its core IT business and also improves continuity of customer contact. By working to agreed standards with service partners, it is able to build long-term customer satisfaction and guarantee effective relationships.

ACTION

- ► **How can you extend the benefits of consultancy service?**
- ► **Can you provide a better service than your specialist competitors?**
- ► **Could you provide the service by managing other suppliers?**
- ► **How can you control the quality of their service?**
- ► **Are you discussing the service with customers at the right level?**

147

Using programme management to strengthen customer relationships

Communications consultancies deliver creative solutions to communications problems and their work is complete when they deliver the print or the video or other communications material. But, unlike advertising agencies or public relations consultancies, they do not have long-term relationships with their customers.

An advertising agency normally has a contract to handle all advertising and associated work for a defined period and is given a budget to cover that. A public relations consultancy is given a similar long-term programme to change attitudes over a period of time for a given fee. Both types of consultancy enjoy continuity of work and they are able to develop long-term relationships with their customers.

BEYOND AD HOC PROJECTS

Communications consultancies, on the other hand, work on an ad hoc basis, handling one project at a time. This is because the industry has grown up from a design and print background where competitive pricing and one-off solutions were the traditional way of working. This did not benefit either party – the communications consultancy could not develop a real understanding of its customer's business and the customer got a series of one-off creative solutions which did not present a consistent image in the marketplace.

IMPLEMENTING THE SOLUTION

Consultants who specialised in corporate identity improved that situation by adding implementation to the original design work. This kept them in contact with customers and also allowed them to control changes at a later stage of the programme.

148

MANAGING PROGRAMMES FOR CUSTOMERS

The computer has added a new dimension by allowing the consultancy to hold and manage information on communications programmes. For example, if a consultancy runs a retail advertising programme, it holds all the information on individual retailers' spending, the results of the investment in advertising and the customers' overall spend. By holding market information on the retailers' sales territories, the consultancy can set up local database marketing programmes which help to improve the precision and cost-effectiveness of marketing.

PROVIDING A MANAGEMENT INFORMATION SERVICE TO CUSTOMERS

The customer receives an efficient management information service which does not tie up his own administrative resources and gains a high level of control over local marketing programmes. This essential service locks the customer into the consultancy. To improve the service even further, the consultancy develops an audit to identify areas of cost saving and efficiency on local marketing programmes. It demonstrates the quality of reporting that can be achieved and shows the customer how management programmes can be further developed.

Programme management allows the consultancy to improve the quality and frequency of contact with the customer and builds an effective relationship that is mutually beneficial.

ACTION

► **Can you identify areas where you can provide programme management services for your customers?**

► **Can you use that service to improve the quality of your customers' business programmes?**

► **How can you ensure that you maintain regular long-term contact with your customers through programme management?**

149

Widening a consultancy discipline

Retail was one of the boom businesses of the 1980s and it encouraged a high level of growth in the design industry. Next, Habitat, BHS (British Home Stores) and other major stores were transformed visually by retail designers, but for many that transformation was superficial – mere window dressing.

A COMPLETE RETAIL SOLUTION

One consultancy however felt it was important to offer retailers a complete solution. A new identity was an integral part of the process because this would signal to the consumer that there was a change in store, but the consultancy also changed the merchandising system, designed new methods of displaying products and even introduced a new product where there was a gap in the range.

It also introduced new training programmes for the staff, because their performance was critical to the success of the transformation. Staff had to understand the new approach to retailing and put it into action. The new approach to retailing focused on high standards of customer service and staff performance was an integral part of that. This was a wide ranging approach to retail development and one that promised effective long-term results. The retail recession has now diverted attention away from the achievements of retail design but that does not affect its underlying principles.

RETAINING CONTACT WITH CUSTOMERS

A depth of involvement like this was vital to developing customer loyalty in a very competitive market. The consultancy faced large numbers of competitors offering retail design solutions, but few of them were offering such broad-ranging business solutions. Typically a consultancy would prepare a pilot design programme and then implement it on a regional or national basis. The consultancy would earn a fee for implementation, as well as design, or it might take an overall fee for managing the project, based on the total value of the programme. But a consultancy's involvement usually ceased after implementation. The scale of a retail design project varied from the redesign of a store fascia to the total implementation of a complete new design on a national scale.

BUILDING CONFIDENCE IN CUSTOMERS

When consultancies wanted to move into the super league, they had to be able to demonstrate their capability across a broad range of disciplines and they had to demonstrate that they had the experience and the resources to manage large-scale projects efficiently. The whole design industry had to build customers' confidence in its professionalism because customers believed they were not capable of implementing the solutions. Traditionally, this work had been handled by architects or interior designers and implemented by shopfitters or the store's own property staff.

CO-OPERATING WITH SPECIALISTS

If consultancies did not have the resources to handle everything themselves, they worked in collaboration with other specialist consultancies and brought together all the resources needed. For example, training companies worked with design companies, while product design and literature design companies collaborated with architects to develop complete solutions.

PRESENTING PROFESSIONALISM

Customer surveys showed that they rated consultants' design skills highly but felt uncomfortable with their management, financial and project skills – design was too often seen as a cottage industry. To convince customers that designers could be effective, consultancies had to go through two stages. They had to demonstrate their design skills – often in competition with other design companies – but then they had to convince the customer that they had the resources to handle implementation professionally. Articles in the design press were a valuable way of showing the quality and depth of work they had achieved. Appointments notices let clients know that they were building and retaining a strong management team which was professional enough to tackle large-scale projects.

151

MAKING DESIGN A STRATEGIC ISSUE

Personal presentation was one of the most important methods of building response. The customer had to be educated in the design process, because there were few professional design managers on the customer side. It was also important to reach the customer at the right level. Retail development on this scale was a major investment, and the design manager was unlikely to have the authority to take that sort of decision – the managing director and the finance director had to give their approval to the project. Presentations were carefully structured to show the real value of the investment decision and convince them that they would be working with effective business partners.

ACTION

▶ **Do you have the resources to provide a complete solution for your customers?**

▶ **Do customers recognise that you provide a complete solution?**

▶ **Are you reviewing project investment at the right level?**

▶ **Do you need to educate your customers in the process of partnership?**

Summary

Professional services are often delivered as a series of one-off projects with no guarantee of continuity of work. Yet both customer and consultancy could benefit from a continuing relationship. This chapter described a number of techniques for building stronger relationships:

- increasing contact through complete business solutions which support your core activities;

- improving your customers' management skills and helping them to enhance their own performance;

- working with your customers' management teams so that you get involved in the development of their business;

- developing your customers' staff so that you build higher levels of customer satisfaction;

- extending consultancy into implementation and maintenance to increase the level of customer contact and account control;

- using programme management to strengthen customer relationships; and

- widening a consultancy discipline to increase the level of customer contact.

This approach to developing business is ideally suited to a service organisation that provides ad hoc services.

14

Information systems

Providing a business solution

Information systems companies have supplied computers to their customers and expected them to make effective use of them. They have not been concerned with the ways in which their customers use the computers.

HELPING CUSTOMERS TO OVERCOME A SKILLS SHORTAGE

Many customers employ their own service staff to support their computer system and their users, developing applications and ensuring that the system is managed effectively. But changing business conditions and a growing shortage of skilled staff means that many companies are not able to provide the level of support that is needed. The systems need to be brought up to date to meet new applications and the companies have to support growing numbers of users. This changing environment provides computer suppliers with an important opportunity to develop stronger relationships with their customers.

PROVIDING CUSTOMERS WITH SKILLS

Within their organisations, the computer companies have skills and resources which can be used by their customers. After-sales service had always been part of a package provided to the customer but the service had been limited to installation and maintenance. Computer companies realised that customers needed a much wider range of services to support their business operations.

OFFERING A COMPLETE SOLUTION

The solution they decided was to offer a total business solution which would meet all the customer's information systems' requirements. This would distance them from competitors who only provided computers and asked the customers to provide all the rest of the support from their own resources. The information systems companies position themselves as business partners who are able to help customers make the most of their investment in information systems.

COMMUNICATING THE STRATEGIC IMPORTANCE OF SERVICES

The strategic approach ensures that information systems services are discussed at a high level. The information systems companies produced executive briefing guides which would explain how information systems helped a company develop its own competitive edge. It also explains the actions the customer needs to take to ensure the best return on its investment. For example, the company demonstrates how the use of external specialist services can improve the competitive edge. This builds commitment and understanding of the business solution at board level and helps to ensure that senior executives understand the real benefits of working with a company that supplies a total solution.

ACTION

▶ **Do your customers depend on scarce skills?**

▶ **Can you provide those skills from your own resources?**

▶ **Do your customers understand how important the services are?**

Adding value to computer services

Computer services have been identified as integral to a total business solution. They supplement the customer's own resources and they help to ensure the customer gets the best return on investment. To be able to offer a total solution, the company must offer services that match each of the customer's requirements and it must be sure that the services represent added value to the customer.

IDENTIFYING ADDED VALUE

Services that are essential to the operation of a product – installation and maintenance – do not represent added value because they do not improve the customer's business performance in any way. By looking at activities that are critical to the customer's success, the computer company has worked out the greatest opportunities for adding value.

IMPROVING CUSTOMERS' DECISION-MAKING

Consultancy for example will help customers improve their own decision-making process so that they can identify the information system that is right for their business requirements. Although consultancy is often delivered by a management consultancy, the company can add further value to the service by providing a detailed understanding of the technical aspects of information systems consultancy.

HELPING CUSTOMERS OVERCOME SKILLS SHORTAGES

Project services help customers set up and operate their computer systems and they can be used to supplement the customer's own resources. There is often a peak workload when a new system is being installed or when a group of new users are brought into the system. The customer support team is fully stretched trying to carry out the new implementation tasks and also keep the existing systems going. If they do not have sufficient resources, the implementation will be delayed and the company may lose competitive advantage. By providing its own skilled people on a short-term basis, the computer company can supplement customers' resources and help to shorten leadtimes. The company demonstrates the cost-effectiveness of using external suppliers by showing how the cost of support services varies with the workload. They also show the short- and long-term cost of recruiting and training specialist computer staff who could then be underutilised when the heavy workload is completed. The services of an external specialist will enable them to meet the short-term requirements.

IMPROVING CUSTOMERS' SKILLS

Training services will ensure that customers have the skills to make the most effective use of their purchase. Although larger customers may have their own training facilities, the computer company can add value through its understanding of the special requirements of computer training.

OFFERING CUSTOMERS ACCESS TO TECHNICAL SKILLS

A computer software programme or application helps customers to carry out a specific business task. In many ways, it is one of the most critical tasks for IT support staff. Unfortunately, the support workload meant that many companies built up a large application development backlog and that limited their progress. By providing access to specialists, the computer company can help the customer develop new applications quickly and improve business performance.

ACTION

► **Can you identify critical tasks which your customers find difficult to handle?**

► **Could you handle those tasks and add extra value?**

► **Which of your services represents greatest value to your customers?**

► **Is there a balance in your business between essential and added-value services?**

Focusing on your customers' markets

A computer company needs to demonstrate that it understands its customers' business needs if it is to work in long-term partnership. This means providing services and products that will support its customers' business processes and not just its equipment. As part of this process, the computer company decides to reorganise its business so that the corporate structure reflects its main markets. The company can then build an understanding of each of these markets and offer a specialist service aligned to the market.

157

IDENTIFYING MARKET SUCCESS FACTORS

A computer company working in the retail sector, for example, knows that it will be working to tight deadlines and that project management and implementation will be critical success factors in the business. A retailer needs to get a computer system up and running quickly so that it can keep stores open. Training is also important because there is a very high turnover of staff and many of the people using the equipment in the retail sector will not be computer-literate; poor performance could lead to low levels of customer satisfaction.

WORKING WITH YOUR CUSTOMERS ON MARKET DEVELOPMENT PROGRAMMES

The computer company can also help customers develop or enhance their own business strategy using computers to build a competitive edge. For example, by setting up a network to collect and distribute information from local retail outlets, the marketing staff at head office can make the branches more responsive to change. Sales and financial information can be analysed daily to identify trends in performance, exploit opportunities and take corrective action where necessary. The customer's head-office team can also try out its own test marketing to see whether particular products or special offers will be helpful in building business. The team can get an immediate feedback on price changes or promotional activity and can then make further local changes or run the campaign nationally. By working closely with customers, the computer company builds a specialised market understanding and demonstrates that it can work as a business partner and help build retail business.

ACTION

- ▶ **Do customers in different market sectors require specific types of service?**
- ▶ **Can you identify the main requirements in each of the sectors?**
- ▶ **Can you meet these requirements with existing services?**
- ▶ **Can you get involved in joint projects with your customers?**

Core services

Core services are the skills and resources a company uses to deliver its services to its customers. Although a customer normally buys the complete product or service, the core services that make up the product can also prove valuable to the customer.

PROVIDING YOUR CUSTOMERS WITH SKILLS AND EXPERIENCE

A computer company handling the processing of credit cards analyses its business and identifies that it has key skills in telephone authorisation, transaction processing, mailing, direct marketing and customer retention. These are skills that can be used by customers to support their own marketing programmes. To develop the skills in his own organisation, a customer would have to make a major investment in recruitment and training. If the customer wants results quickly, there may not be time to wait. The computer company offers an off-the-shelf solution which will provide rapid results without a major investment.

STRENGTHENING BUSINESS RELATIONSHIPS

These core skills help the customer develop his own business and help to strengthen the business relationship. The core services marketing programme helps to broaden the base of the business and also provides a valuable source of incremental income.

PROVIDING THE RIGHT LEVEL OF SERVICE

It is important to maintain a balance between marketing core services and using them to deliver your own product or service. If too many of your resources are tied up in providing external services, your ability to maintain your own standards of service could be affected. You also need to ensure that your staff understand customer service. They see themselves as an internal service department not affected by business pressures. Now they have to work under pressure to recognised standards and they have to develop positive attitudes of customer care. An internal communications programme will help to develop the right attitudes and will demonstrate that the company is committed to the success of the core skills programme.

159

ACTION

▶ **Can you identify core skills that your customers could utilise?**

▶ **Do you have the capacity to market these services outside your company?**

▶ **Would these services add value to your relationship with the customer?**

Summary

Computer companies have followed the lead of professional

service organisations and used services to build loyalty. The sales cycle for information systems is long and it is vital that suppliers maintain contact between sales. This chapter described the strategy which includes:

- providing a business solution which helps customers achieve the best return on their investment in computer systems;
- adding value to computer systems by helping customers improve their own business performance;
- focusing on your customers' markets so that services reflect the specialist needs of different market sectors; and
- offering customers your core services so that you add further value to the relationship.

This aspect of the computer business has become so important that many computer companies are repositioning themselves as service organisations.

15

Retaining customer loyalty in a car dealership

The importance of maintaining contact between sales

Customer retention poses special problems for car manufacturers and their franchised dealers; people change their cars every two to three years on average and there may be little formal contact between customer and dealer during that time. When customers think about choosing their next car, they will probably have forgotten how the dealer treated them last time and they may be easily swayed by special offers from competitors.

Dealers have to find a way to increase contact and build loyalty during the period between sales so that their dealership is the customer's first point of contact when he or she comes to choose the next car.

One way to increase contact is to encourage the customer to return to the dealership for service and repairs or spare parts but, with increasing competition from independent parts and service operations, this is not an easy task. Dealers have to prove that they are competitive and they must offer a service that is visibly different from the independents – a service that builds the highest levels of satisfaction. If customers are satisfied with every aspect of dealer service, they are likely to give that dealership favourable consideration for future car purchases. This is known in the car business as achieving satisfaction throughout the ownership experience.

This chapter gives examples of a number of programmes and actions that help to build loyalty with private and business car owners.

ACTION

► **How can you maintain contact with your customers when they only buy your products every two to three years?**

► **Are you making full use of aftersales operations to maintain contact with customers?**

► **How can you distinguish your aftersales operations from competitors?**

► **Have you considered your aftersales operations as part of 'a complete ownership experience?'**

Making the most of parts and service operations

In the car industry, as in many other businesses, parts and service are proving to be the critical element in customer retention because they provide the greatest opportunity for customer contact. It is essential that parts and service staff understand customer needs and have the backing of marketing programmes to help retain customers.

Unfortunately, staff in those departments have been used to simply responding to customer requests – formerly there was no pressure on them actively to sell their services. But, as new and used car sales revenues have declined, the traditional franchised dealership parts and service business has been attacked on a number of fronts – by national chains of parts specialists and independent parts and service outlets who offer competitive prices and fast service on a narrow range of popular parts and repairs such as tyres, exhausts or batteries.

When the independents turned to scheduled servicing, they applied the same principles of competitive prices, popular product lines, fast stock turn and heavy consumer advertising combined with an attractive retail layout. The independents positioned themselves as the cost-effective and convenient alternative to the manufacturers' franchised dealerships.

This was not a serious problem when new car sales were strong -owners had to use the dealership servicing facilities during the period of new car warranty – but, when new car sales declined, dealers found that owners were keeping their vehicles longer, and they were not bringing them back to the dealership for service. The independent outlets appeared to offer a service that was better suited to owners of older cars – low prices, convenient modular service that covered the most popular jobs and a drive-in, no appointment facility.

The onus was on the franchised dealers to sell their parts and service operations to regain lost business and maintain contact with customers. The manufacturers' response was to analyse the changing nature of the market and develop a range of services which would win back specific types of business.

163

DEMONSTRATING THE CONVENIENCE OF THE DEALERSHIP SERVICE

Manufacturers identified that convenience was a major factor in encouraging customers to choose a service outlet. They encouraged dealers to extend their opening hours, improve parking, speed up the reception process and simplify their pricing structure.

OWNERS OUTSIDE WARRANTY

To appeal to owners outside warranty, they offered an extended warranty which guaranteed free replacement of major car parts, provided the owners had the car regularly serviced by the dealer. This helped dealers to retain service customers by offering them peace of mind and a higher resale value for their car.

OWNERS OF OLDER CARS

An increasing number of owners no longer bought scheduled servicing – either they did it themselves or they neglected their cars. Research showed that this type of owner was most concerned about price and quality, so the manufacturer responded by offering a guarantee for life on a broad range of repairs and replacement parts fitted by the dealership. This increased service business and built loyalty by giving the customer peace of mind.

WINNING BACK CUSTOMERS FROM COMPETITORS

To ensure that lost customers were aware of the quality and value of the dealership service, manufacturers operated local price-based advertising campaigns which highlighted dealer offers on popular parts and service.

164

ENCOURAGING PROSPECTS TO TRY THE DEALERSHIP SERVICE

To encourage owners to try the dealership service, they offered free safety checks and seasonal checks such as 'Getting your car ready for winter'. This not only demonstrated customer care, but also gave dealers the opportunity to identify service work and build incremental income.

These programmes helped to build business for the parts and service department and, most important, gave the dealership the opportunity to build customer satisfaction and loyalty throughout the ownership period.

ACTION

▶ **How often do your customers need replacement parts or service during their period of ownership?**

▶ **How can you ensure that your customers use your company or your franchised dealers for parts and service?**

► **How efficiently can you offer parts and service compared with your competitors?**

► **What factors do customers regard as important when they buy parts and service?**

Introducing retail techniques to a supply business

Car manufacturers recognise that, if they are going to appeal to consumers, they must operate as retailers and not as manufacturers selling through dealers. Consumers have higher expectations of customer service following the retail developments of the 1980s and many car dealerships have yet to catch up.

The parts department, for example, is usually a trade counter where people ask for a specific part and queue patiently while staff vanish into a warehouse to look for the product. Although customers may get the products they want, there is no opportunity for suggesting additional purchase or encouraging impulse purchase.

165

A department like this is ripe for retail development. With a growing population of women drivers and younger drivers owning older vehicles, there are two main opportunities:

- sell accessories; and
- meet the needs of the do-it-yourself market.

In both cases, a retail environment is vital; customers want to be free to browse among accessories and DIY products. These are often impulse purchases and the total value of the order is likely to increase with the right retail approach. A 'parts shop' is designed as a retail outlet rather than a trade counter and it features attractive self-service product displays.

ENCOURAGING RETAIL DEVELOPMENT

It takes a major change to create a retail environment within a parts department and to encourage staff to sell and utilise merchandising techniques, rather than just respond to requests over the counter. Dealers have to be convinced that it is worth giving up valuable space in the dealership and making the necessary investment in new products and merchandising material to shift those products.

LAUNCHING A RETAIL PROGRAMME

To launch the concept, manufacturers run a pilot programme in a number of dealerships and then use testimonials to promote the programme nationally at a series of regional meetings.

IMPLEMENTING THE PROGRAMME

A comprehensive operating guide gives each dealership the practical information it needs to set up its own 'parts shop' and this is backed by a design advisory service which can be used to plan a specific shop for the dealership.

DEVELOPING DEALERSHIP STAFF SKILLS

Training staff in merchandising techniques, product knowledge and customer care is an important part of retail development, together with guidelines on recruiting appropriate staff for the shop.

PROVIDING CUSTOMER INFORMATION

To ensure that customers are aware of the shop, it needs to be extensively advertised. Consumer literature also becomes important to ensure customers have information on the products and services available.

EXTENDING THE RETAIL CONCEPT TO SERVICE

The retail concept can be extended to the service department. This means rethinking the way service is sold and introducing concepts such as menu pricing so that customers can buy a series of clearly defined products such as a brake service, an electronic engine check-up, or a tyre replacement for a specific price. Menu pricing is designed to reduce the uncertainty with 'a price you see is the price you pay' promise on a wide range of specified services. This is equivalent to buying services in a shop and helps to create a retail environment in the service department.

Developments like this help to improve the standards of customer care in a parts and service department and encourage customers to return to the dealership for casual browsing. This builds informal contact and offers opportunities for repeat purchase.

ACTION

- ► **How can you apply retailing techniques to your parts and service operations?**
- ► **How can you use retailing to build customer loyalty?**
- ► **Have you integrated sales training and merchandising in your retail development programme?**

Improving convenience for customers

Car manufacturers want to ensure that their customers always enjoy peace of mind. Customers realise that their cars may break down occasionally, but they can be reassured that help is at hand if anything goes wrong.

Motoring organisations were among the first to introduce the concept of assured mobility. They provided a rescue service to carry out roadside repairs and, if they couldn't repair the car themselves, they took it to the nearest garage. This went a stage further when they introduced a recovery service which would take customers back to their home or on to their next destination.

A further refinement was the introduction of other options for getting to the next destination. For example, the customer could stay overnight in a hotel or go onto the next destination by public transport or by hire car while the broken-down vehicle was repaired. In all cases, the idea was to keep the customer moving in the event of a breakdown.

SUPPORTING CUSTOMERS DURING A BREAKDOWN

Car manufacturers have realised that this concept of complete mobility provides reassurance for their own customers, so membership of one of the motoring organisations is now a regular part of the new car package. Manufacturers also include this option in their extended warranty programmes. The customer signs an agreement for two or three years which gives free parts and labour coverage in the event of a breakdown. As part of the incentive to take out the package, they also include membership of a motoring organisation.

168

MAKING SCHEDULED SERVICE MORE CONVENIENT

Surveys indicate that convenience is one of the strongest factors influencing customers' choice of car servicing. Any action that could reduce inconvenience would help to increase customer satisfaction. A number of manufacturers have introduced a courtesy vehicle programme to keep customers mobile while their cars are in the workshop for service or repair.

By reducing the inconvenience for their customers, dealers can attract business away from competitors who trade only on price. This type of programme demonstrates high levels of customer care and may be a crucial factor when customers are reviewing a manufacturer's total offering.

ACTION

- ▶ **Do your customers suffer inconvenience when their products are being repaired?**
- ▶ **Can you offer customers substitute products or services during the repair period?**
- ▶ **Can you improve the quality of your warranty by introducing services to reduce inconvenience?**

Winning back lost service customers

With the decline in new car sales, manufacturers are putting greater emphasis on sales of older cars and providing the right type of service operation to retain the loyalty of owners of older cars. This is a difficult task because owners of older cars tend to carry out their own repairs and servicing or use lower-cost sources such as independent garages or mobile mechanics.

BUILDING TRUST IN THE DEALERSHIP

Used car dealers don't enjoy the best of reputations, so to reassure customers and demonstrate customer care, a number of manufacturers provide guaranteed used vehicles which have been thoroughly prepared and serviced by their franchised dealers. Other manufacturers have taken the concept further and are using national advertising to promote either their own used cars or other makes of cars prepared by their dealers. They are setting up centres dedicated to the sale and service of older cars.

169

BUILDING A NEW APPROACH IN THE DEALERSHIP

Winning back lost customers may require some physical changes to the dealership such as separate used car sales areas and greater space for servicing, bodyshop and sales of reconditioned parts.

IMPROVING CONTACT

It takes a major effort in customer follow-up to ensure that manufacturer and dealers regain contact with older customers.

Most manufacturers and dealers maintain contact through the warranty period but then lose contact. If a customer buys a car from a non-franchised dealer, the manufacturer's opportunity to make contact is even smaller. However by setting up specific services aimed at older car owners, they can reintroduce them to the dealership experience. For example, free safety checks or special service offers targeted at older vehicles will help to attract customers back.

OFFERING SPECIAL SERVICES

Pricing, convenience and flexibility are the key factors in winning back lost service customers, and a number of dealers are introducing a new service structure to compete effectively. They are reducing their labour rates, opening at special times like Saturday mornings and operating modified servicing to suit owners of older cars.

SETTING UP ALTERNATIVE SERVICE OPERATIONS

Surveys show that manufacturers' service operations are regarded as expensive and poor value for money. To overcome those objections, a number of manufacturers are setting up independent servicing operations which operate under a different name.

RAISING STANDARDS IN THE OLDER CAR MARKET

Whatever preliminary action is taken it is important to provide the highest standards of service to older car customers. This will encourage them to continue using the dealership and build their loyalty.

HELPING DEALERS WIN BACK THE CUSTOMERS

Make sure your dealers understand the need to attract this type of work, explain the opportunities in the market and show how dealers can attract prospects. Advertising and promotion play an important part, so it is important to provide a full support service.

Winning back lost service business not only increases income and profit, it builds contact with a group of potential car buyers and gives the dealership the opportunity to build effective long-term relationships.

ACTION

▶ **Can you identify why you are losing service business to competitors?**

▶ **Why do prospects choose competitors?**

▶ **How can you modify your service to meet the needs of lost customers?**

▶ **Can you set up alternative service operations that would be more appealing to lost customers?**

Supporting volume customers through distributors

Fleet operators who purchase cars in volume represent a major market for car manufacturers and dealers. Fleet sales are critical to the success and profitability of a mass market car and when a new car is being launched it is often designed and marketed with the fleet operator in mind.

When fleet operators choose a manufacturer they are looking at a number of factors:

- broad model range to cover all the requirements in the fleet from senior executive to sales representative and delivery driver;

- prestige, to add perceived value to the car;

- good resale value; and

- simple maintenance and low operating costs.

The battle for customer loyalty in the fleet market is fiercely contested because a fleet loss can significantly affect a manufacturer's turnover and profitability. Although dealers play a minor role in determining the choice of cars, the service they provide to fleet operators can be a crucial factor in building long-term satisfaction and loyalty.

171

GIVING FLEET OPERATORS CONSISTENT NATIONWIDE SERVICE

Fleet operators need to know that they can obtain a consistent standard of service wherever their vehicles are located. Fleet drivers may cover the entire country, so a nationwide service could be important. It is essential that every dealer in the network provides the same standard of service; one problem dealership can reflect badly on the rest of the network.

OPERATING COST-EFFECTIVE SERVICING PROGRAMMES

Service programmes are carefully developed to ensure the lowest cost of ownership and reduce overall operating costs. Encourage dealers to negotiate special contracts with fleet owners to provide volume discounts on servicing costs.

172

MAKING FLEET SERVICING MORE CONVENIENT

They can also provide special service facilities such as overnight servicing, replacement vehicles or on-site servicing which helps to keep the vehicles in the fleet on the move. This represents value for money because a fleet that is on the move is earning its keep.

SUPPORTING FLEET OPERATORS' OWN WORKSHOPS

Many fleet operators run their own service operations and they depend on a ready stock of replacement parts, with the back-up of an emergency delivery service. Dealers who provide a parts service to fleet workshops also provide an advisory service to help fleet customers plan and manage their own parts department.

PROVIDING FLEETS WITH OPERATING INFORMATION

The information available from dealership parts and service departments can be used to provide fleets with a valuable guide to their operating costs. By putting this information onto computer and providing fleet customers with access, the dealer can help fleet operators manage their vehicles more efficiently, and this can help to maintain loyalty to the manufacturer.

It is important that dealers understand the importance of the fleet market. Their own car sales are not affected because major fleet sales are handled directly by the manufacturer, but fleet parts and service sales represent good, regular revenue and profit opportunities.

ACTION

- ▶ **Can you identify volume service opportunities among fleet or national customers?**
- ▶ **Would special service activities help to build loyalty in the fleet market?**
- ▶ **Can you utilise information on service and repairs to provide your customers with operating information?**

173

Supporting smaller business users

The term fleet operations is usually applied to companies running large numbers of vehicles, but there may be other business users running their own vehicles or small fleets who could benefit from a fleet-type service and provide dealers with a regular customer base. This group includes:

- individual business drivers living away from fleet headquarters;
- small firms with a few vehicles;
- owner-drivers running small businesses;
- self-employed people; and
- individuals who depend on their vehicle to carry out their business.

Like the fleet operator, business drivers are looking for convenience and reliability in the service they receive from dealerships but they are also looking for a long-term relationship so that they can have peace of mind that they will get the right level of attention in the event of a problem.

A SPECIAL SERVICE FOR BUSINESS USERS

A number of manufacturers and dealers are setting up a specialist service to cater for business users. They know that they cannot afford to be without their vehicle for any specific length of time, so they provide special facilities such as overnight servicing, collection and delivery service or replacement vehicles to ensure that the business driver stays mobile. Courtesy vehicles, for example, not only minimise inconvenience, they show that the dealership regards the customer's business as important.

IMPROVING ADMINISTRATION

174

Independent garages and servicing chains have attracted business users away from franchised dealers through competitive pricing and careful invoicing. Franchised dealers, on the other hand, have been criticised for administrative problems such as failing to contact customers about additional work and then presenting bills which exceed the original estimate. Customers stay loyal when they are confident they are getting value for money.

Customers who depend on their cars for their livelihood recognise the contribution that good service makes to their business. By providing them with the highest standards of care, you can ensure that they depend on your dealers and that builds a loyal customer base.

ACTION

► **Have you got clearly defined standards of service for your business customers?**

► **Can you identify groups of customers who depend on quality service?**

► **Do your service standards focus on customer convenience?**

Community programmes

Sometimes customer loyalty grows through unexpected channels. Community programmes, for example, can help to demonstrate customer care and attract a wider audience, as well as media attention.

Car-care courses for women are a good example of a high profile event which can raise public awareness of a dealership. With a growing population of women motorists – now about 40 per cent of the driving population – there is a demand for information on car care and safety.

ATTRACTING THE PUBLIC AS WELL AS CUSTOMERS

A number of manufacturers have met the need by running broad-ranging car-confidence workshops which help women understand their car, demonstrate basic maintenance and provide useful information on vehicle and personal safety. The events intentionally attract a much broader audience than just dealership customers but, because there is no sales pressure at the event, the visitors may turn out to be valuable sales and service prospects.

FOLLOWING UP COMMUNITY PROGRAMMES

The experience of dealers who have organised events like this is that they help to raise awareness of customer service standards and that builds long-term relationships. Many of the visitors can turn out to be advocates of the dealership because they have been well treated. Obtain the names and addresses of all the visitors as the basis for a direct-mail follow-up campaign.

ATTRACTING OTHER GROUPS

Women are one key group, but events can also be run for pensioners, disabled motorists, young drivers or other groups such as people who have recently purchased a new car. Each of

these events can help to raise high levels of interest and awareness in the community.

SUPPORTING COMMUNITY EVENTS

Programmes like this require three levels of support:

- launch material which explains the concept, benefits and principles of the programme;
- an operating guide which gives step-by-step guidelines on
  organising an event; and
- merchandising material to support the event.

ACTION

► **Do your products and services have a wider appeal in the community?**

► **Do your services demonstrate high levels of customer care?**

► **Do your dealers need support in organising community events?**

176

Summary

Customers rarely change their cars until the second or third year
of ownership and that makes it difficult for manufacturers and
dealers to maintain effective contact between sales. Car manufacturers have led the way in operating customer loyalty programmes, and this chapter showed examples of their approach:

- making the most of parts and service operations to attract
  customers to the dealership;
- introducing retailing techniques to a supply business to
  increase the level of contact;
- improving convenience for customers to build higher levels of
  satisfaction;
- winning back lost service customers by running a series of
  loyalty-building promotional offers;

- supporting volume customers through distributors by offering service and management support;
- supporting business users by offering them higher levels of convenience; and
- operating community programmes to increase the opportunity for informal contact.

Programmes like these can help companies selling consumer or business products with long sales cycles.

177

16

Financial institutions

Building customers for life

'Customers for life' is not a new concept for banks or building societies but, in the fiercely competitive financial services market, it has taken on a new dimension. Traditionally, few people changed their bank accounts or building society unless there were serious problems but the blurring of the edges between the two has increased the choice. At one time, banks were for current accounts and building societies for savings and home loans, but both institutions now offer similar services.

This is partly due to a change in financial regulations and partly the result of increased competition. Both institutions are trying to attract the same customers and, when they have attracted them, they are looking at ways of retaining them. The aim is to meet the changing needs of customers through life by offering a broad portfolio of products.

COMPETING THROUGH CUSTOMER SERVICE

The attack is on two fronts – to provide the highest standards of service and to develop an evolving range of products to meet all their customers' needs. Service is a combination of two factors – the technology to support effective account administration and the use of technology to build relationships.

USING TECHNOLOGY TO IMPROVE PERSONAL SERVICE

Banks and building societies have made a major investment in technology to automate many of the back-office functions and free staff to concentrate on building relationships with customers. The same technology can be used to improve front-office functions and the personal service given to customers. For example, by holding all customer information on computer, staff can speed up the response to a customer enquiry and can demonstrate higher standards of customer care because they do not have to ask customers for routine details.

BUILDING RELATIONSHIPS

The same information can be used to develop a personal portfolio of services for individual customers. Database information is a vital element in building customer profiles and tailoring services to them. It is also important that staff know how to use this information to build customer relations so training is a vital element in the mix. The customers' expectations should not be dashed when they come to a branch for service.

MAINTAINING CONTACT WITH CUSTOMERS

Advertising campaigns reflecting the 'customers for life' theme explain to customers how the bank or building society will meet their changing requirements. Regular mailing programmes will help to keep customers up to date with the changing product and service profile and will enable them to exploit direct marketing opportunities.

BUILDING UNDERSTANDING IN THE BRANCHES

To introduce the service to local branches and to get the commitment of staff, a launch guide explains the principles of 'customers for life'. It shows who in the branch will be involved and how the responsibilities will be apportioned. The guide should describe the benefits of the programme and explain the communications that support it.

ACTION

▸ **Do you understand how your customers' needs change through their lives?**

▸ **Is the concept of 'customers for life' appropriate to your business?**

▸ **Have you got the information you need to build relationships with individual customers?**

▸ **Are you using technology to improve service and build relationships?**

Using card marketing to segment the market

Card marketing can be an excellent way to build and maintain customer loyalty. Cards offer issuers important information about their customers and their spending patterns and this can act as an effective base for direct marketing.

FLEXIBLE RESPONSE TO CUSTOMER CHANGE

The important thing about cards is that the market can be segmented. Card products can be enhanced and value added to give the customer additional benefits. By segmenting the card, upgrading it and continually refining it to the changing needs of the customer, the bank can reinforce the concept of 'customers for life'. For example, a higher income earner can be given a gold card which has higher credit limits or relevant privileges.

SEGMENTING THE MARKET

Banks have traditionally issued a single standard card which has one level of issue but with different levels of expenditure. However, competition in the credit card market means that other card issuers are capturing their traditional business and affecting customer retention programmes. The introduction of charges for credit card users significantly changed the marketplace and placed even greater emphasis on customer loyalty programmes.

INTRODUCING NEW CARD PRODUCTS

The banks responded by introducing a wider range of card products aimed at different sectors of the market. They also encouraged higher levels of use and spending by rewarding customers for frequent use. These frequent user programmes provide customers with high value gifts as an incentive to stay loyal.

ACTION

▶ **Would market segmentation enable you to compete more effectively?**

▶ **Can you convert your standard products to niche products?**

Financial advice   181

Impartial advice can help to demonstrate high levels of customer care and increase sales of financial products. Insurance companies and independent financial advisers have long used this as a technique for introducing services and maintaining contact.

TAILORING A SERVICE

Financial health checks are used to build up a profile of the customer and to develop a personal portfolio tailored to that customer's needs. It fits in with the corporate strategy of developing customers for life and providing a personal financial service.

BUILDING UNDERSTANDING OF THE SERVICE

Because the programme is so critical to customer loyalty, it is launched at a high level to get the commitment of the branch manager. Branches have to understand that they are in the business of providing advice and guidance, not just running current account operations. They have to employ qualified staff to provide the right levels of advice, they need the right portfolio of products and services and they need to convince customers that they are in the business of providing independent financial advice.

ACQUIRING THE RIGHT SKILLS

Providing the right level of professional advice and guidance may require an investment in recruiting or retraining specialist staff. An alternative is to work in association with a specialist company.

TELLING CUSTOMERS ABOUT THE SERVICE

The customer base provides a good starting point for launching the service. The service can be offered initially to higher income customers, people who are higher rate deposit account holders for example, or holders of the bank's gold credit card.

ACTION

- ▶ **Can you provide advice and guidance to your customers?**
- ▶ **Have you got the skills and resources to provide the service?**
- ▶ **Can you work with specialist companies to provide the service?**

Offering customers greater choice

One of the ways in which a financial institution can increase its market penetration is to segment the market and develop specific products for each sector. In practical terms, that means looking through the bank's customer base and levels of business.

MODIFYING SERVICES

The current account market looks simple at first glance, but the high street banks found that they could offer customers different types of service which matched their requirements. One of the simplest changes was to add interest to current account balances, so that customers who maintain their accounts in credit could actually take advantage of that. Offering tiered levels of interest helped to attract higher income earners and increased the overall customer base.

USING CUSTOMER INFORMATION TO MODIFY SERVICES

The second stage was to build in an automatic overdraft facility for creditworthy customers. This minimised inconvenience for the customer, reduced administration for the bank and showed a higher level of customer care. This ability to offer built-in overdrafts allowed them to target different income groups. A further variation was the introduction of a built-in agreement to provide personal loans up to a certain limit. Pre-arranged loans and overdrafts gave the banks a much higher level of flexibility and allowed them to tailor the facilities to specific groups of customers.

183

PACKAGING RELATED SERVICES

To segment the market even further, customers were offered different packaged versions of current accounts. Three versions were available – one for customers who occasionally overdrew and needed flexibility, one for customers who always maintained a good balance in their current accounts and one for customers whose accounts fluctuated regularly. Each account includes different services and these can be tailored to individual customers.

EXPANDING THE MARKET

The savings market gave a further opportunity to segment the market. Savers already have a choice of schemes offering different rates and withdrawal methods, but there were a number of gaps in the market, particularly at the lower end where prospects were put off by the high minimal deposit required. There was a great deal of development work to attract small savers and this also helped to broaden the customer base. By offering a wider range of services to groups of customers who normally fell outside the net, the banks were able to improve the quality and frequency of customer contact.

MAKING STAFF AWARE OF THE NEW SERVICES

Information on the different products and services is communicated to customers through product literature and consumer advertising. One of the major problems was getting branch staff to understand the difference between the various accounts and helping them to identify prospects for each of these services. Product training is an essential part of the launch programme.

ACTION

► **Can you increase the overall market by introducing new products?**

► **Can you package services to appeal to specific groups of customers?**

Increasing customer convenience

High street banks have introduced a number of methods for making banking more convenient for their customers. They have installed cash dispensers to handle simple transactions like cash withdrawals, deposits and statements outside banking hours or away from the main banking counters. A number of these dispensers are now installed in separate halls so that customers do not have to wait in longer queues and they can shelter in security from the weather. Building societies and other financial institutions have linked together to provide a nationwide network of cash dispensers for their customers.

EXTENDING CONVENIENCE TO OTHER SERVICES

If customers want to use other bank services, however, they are still reliant on access to the bank. Some banks have responded with longer opening hours, particularly on Saturdays, to compete with the building societies. There is also selected opening in the evenings at larger branches, where either a full or limited range of services is on offer. One bank introduced a 24-hour telephone bank which was manned all the time so that customers could phone up with queries and could give instructions for certain transactions such as standing orders or funds transfers.

PUTTING BANKING IN THE HOME

The introduction of home banking can give customers a great deal of control over the way their accounts are run. A modem allows the customer to access the bank's computer to obtain information on his or her own account. The information can be displayed on a personal computer so that the customer can analyse information and get an up-to-date picture. The customer can also send specific instructions on making payments or making transfers. Information on bank products can be requested easily so this makes it a powerful direct marketing tool which allows the bank to communicate with its customers.

185

HELPING CUSTOMERS WITH TECHNOLOGY

These services will help to build long-term relationships – the links tend to tie the customer to the bank and decrease the likelihood of the account moving. In many cases banks can loan or give their customers the equipment and provide instructions to ensure that they are comfortable with it.

ACTION

► **Can you change your opening hours or offer other services to improve convenience?**

► **Are you using technology to deliver standard services?**

► **Can you provide your customers with the technology to increase convenience?**

Providing support for small businesses

As part of its support programme for small businesses, the banks have developed a wide range of services. At the heart of these is a customer charter which shows how the bank will deal with its customers. The banks have acquired a poor reputation because of their treatment of small businesses during the recession. They were accused of lending freely in times of easy money and then putting pressure on businesses when there were problems.

SETTING OUT STANDARDS FOR CUSTOMERS

The charter explains the basis on which the banks will conduct their business, how their charges are levied and how they will notify customers in the event of any problems. The charter is an essential element in building the right sort of relationship and attracting and retaining new customers.

IMPROVING THE QUALITY OF ADVICE TO CUSTOMERS

Much of the banks' earlier efforts had been spent on attracting new business by promoting the start-up services they offered. One of the major problems with any small business is that it is usually low on financial expertise. In fact many new businesses fail in the first year so the banks had an opportunity to provide a level of expertise and guidance which could be extremely valuable to small businesses. Most banks have small business advisers who can provide an individual tailored service, but it is important that the adviser understands the problems and opportunities of small businesses and can relate to them personally.

PROVIDING CUSTOMERS WITH BUSINESS INFORMATION

The personal adviser is backed up with a broad range of information publications which provide detailed advice on finance-related issues such as cash flow, budgeting, taxation and accounting practices. The best publications offer practical advice in a usable form, for example, workbooks or software programs which the customer can use to develop their own skills.

BUILDING RELATIONSHIPS

The personal advice and guidance also gives the bank the opportunity to understand the customers' business and tailor product and services to individual requirements. Organising seminars and other events on topics of interest to small businesses is another way to demonstrate professionalism and build valuable relationships.

ACTION

▶ **Can you support inexperienced customers with advice and guidance?**

▶ **Are you helping your customers to grow their own business?**

▶ **Do your customers understand how you do business with them?**

Matching financial services to customers' needs

When banks issue credit cards to their corporate customers, they have an opportunity to segment the market and build effective business relations with them. Corporate credit cards offer customers the means to control their spending on travel and entertainment, simplify administration and improve their cash flow. By segmenting the business users' market the banks can increase their market penetration and offer their corporate customers a higher value service which will also build long-term business relationships.

PUTTING CUSTOMERS IN CHARGE OF SPENDING

Corporate cards provide different levels of reporting and control and this can be tailored to a customer's requirements. For example a small building firm which has used credit cards for purchasing supplies and petrol decides to issue ordinary credit cards to some of its supervisory staff. This will reduce the burden of petty cash and provide easier information for the accounts.

HELPING CUSTOMERS IMPROVE FINANCIAL CONTROL

An engineering firm with a large nationwide sales force and a series of regional sales offices is looking for ways to increase control over its sales force costs at regional and national level. The bank is able to develop a statement structure so that the local office gets a summary and individual statements for all its own staff for control purposes and a complete version is sent to the head office for settlement. The various sales managers and financial controllers are able to analyse the statements and identify areas where further control needs to be exercised. The bank is also able to issue a traders' summary which shows where the money is being spent. It identifies hotel groups, restaurants and petrol companies which are regularly used. By adding up the expenditure and negotiating volume discounts with preferred suppliers, the company is able to reduce its overall sales force expenditure. The bank has therefore been able to contribute to the improvement of a business process.

OFFERING CUSTOMERS FLEXIBLE OPTIONS

Another way in which the bank can help the business is to offer a range of credit cards under one administrative scheme.

- Salesmen, for example, could get a card which is restricted to petrol, entertainment and travel accommodation.
- Delivery drivers could get a petrol only charge card.
- Directors and senior managers could get a higher status card which has higher spending limits and a number of privileges attached to it. For example, executives travelling abroad could get the benefit of a travel club or travel lounge and a card which is internationally accepted. The company might also get discounts on its travel bills and free travel insurance.

STRENGTHENING BUSINESS RELATIONSHIPS

To build stronger relationships with major customers, the bank developed computerised reporting systems which ran on the bank's own computers or were sold as software to the customers. The bank also offered an annual review of the customers' credit card portfolio to see whether it still met the business management requirements. The information management and control this provided helped to position the bank as a business partner.

ACTION

▶ **Do you understand the different ways your customers use your products or services?**

▶ **Can you tailor your products or services to meet those differing needs?**

▶ **Can you add management control to your products or services?**

189

Supporting your customers with your international experience

A bank with a global branch network can provide valuable international business experience for its customers, particularly if they are trying to develop their own export activities. The bank's knowledge of local market conditions can help to prevent costly mistakes, while its understanding of currency and payments requirements means that it can provide the company with valuable financial expertise.

PROVIDING LOCAL MARKET EXPERTISE

A global bank has built up a network of branches throughout the world and develops an expertise in the main industrial markets. Key staff are given wide-ranging international experience to build their expertise before moving into a consultancy role. In its presentations to customers, the bank stresses its comprehensive network of offices, and the expertise it has developed. The bank supports its customers' activities by running seminars for export marketing staff and also explains the procedures customers will have to adopt to do business in any particular territory. This helps customers define their own requirements and to apply the right management skills.

ACTION

► **Can you provide your customers with specific market expertise?**

► **Can you help to develop the skills of their staff?**

190 Giving customers the benefits of your technology

When the major banks invested in electronic banking, they realised that this would allow them to build even stronger links with corporate customers. By giving customers access to electronic banking technology, banks can provide them with processes and systems that will help the customers develop a competitive edge. Customers gain access to the bank's international networks and systems for carrying out transactions and processing information and they do not have to invest in their own network.

HELPING CUSTOMERS IDENTIFY THEIR OWN NEEDS

Electronic banking replaces a large volume of paper-based transactions and can speed up the process and efficiency of financial administration. The banks perceive that larger companies with many branches – particularly international operations – will benefit most from moving money around quickly and easily. To demonstrate the benefits, they prepare a business case which shows how transactions processing can be simplified by replacing paper with computer-based transactions. The presentation shows how the terminals can be linked to the company's existing computer networks to integrate the accounting processes. To help the company benefit from electronic banking, they analyse the skills and training requirement, helping the company to install any necessary equipment and familiarising staff with the new procedures. Because new users may not be familiar with the systems, the banks offer an advice and guidance helpline to re-assure customers that they are fully supported.

HELPING CUSTOMERS MAKE THE MOST OF THE TECHNOLOGY

The next stage is to show customers how to make the best use of electronic banking to improve their competitive edge. Here the bank uses its experience of working with other businesses to provide a consultancy service to customers. This consultancy service takes the banks beyond the role of supplier and into one of business partner. As customers re-align their business strategies to take advantage of the electronic banking network, they become increasingly dependent on a continuing relationship with the bank.

191

ADDING OTHER NETWORK FACILITIES FOR CUSTOMERS

As well as handling banking transactions, the banks can also offer their customers the use of the network for routine transactions. For example, a company with branch offices around the country can use the data network to communicate sales and financial information between branches and head office. The data network can also be used by customers to set up an interchange network with retailers to handle credit card authorisation, accounting, pricing, and other forms of settlement. This helps the company achieve greater efficiency without investing in a network or the skills to manage it.

ACTION

▶ **Could customers make use of your investment in technology?**

► **Do you have the capacity to provide customer access to your systems?**

► **Can you use your expertise in technology to provide consultancy to your customers?**

► **Can you sell services to help your customers make use of your technology?**

► **Can you customise your technology to meet your customers' needs?**

Summary

Financial institutions have an opportunity to build 'customers for life'. By analysing their customers' changing needs, they can develop a range of products and services that continue to meet those changing needs. This chapter described how a combination of product development and personal service was helping to achieve this. The techniques included:

- operating 'customers for life' programmes;
- using card marketing to segment the market and maintain customer loyalty at a number of different levels;
- offering customers greater choice and packaging services to appeal to specific groups of customers;
- increasing customer convenience by using appropriate new technology;
- providing support for small businesses by improving the quality of advice and improving standards of service;
- matching financial services to customers' needs to increase dependence;
- giving customers the benefits of your technology to build stronger relationships; and
- helping customers build international business by offering your experience and skills.

The concept of 'customers for life' can be applied to many different types of business, particularly those that have opportunities for high levels of customer contact.

17

Developing loyalty in the retail sector

Improving the quality of staff

'This store is closed for staff training every Wednesday morning for half an hour. We do this so that we can offer our customers a higher standard of service'.

This says to customers that a retailer is concerned about the quality of service it offers. Staff training can often be an invisible process and the results may not be obvious. In fact, the better the training the less obvious it will be because nothing goes wrong.

RECRUITING THE RIGHT STAFF

A continuous commitment to training improves a retailer's ability to recruit and retain staff. People are looking for jobs with opportunity and potential, so make sure your job advertisements and your recruitment literature explain the training that is available. In your induction programmes, help people to understand their future career paths and show them how your training programme will help them achieve their goals.

PROVIDE RELEVANT TRAINING

Staff development can take various forms – training in customer care, product information or personal skills to improve the quality of service. Use external training resources to supplement your own skills. There is a vast range of standard training material including videos on customer care, retail industry training programmes, product information from suppliers and retail programmes from specialist training companies. Before you select a package, look closely at your business because it is your customers' needs that shape your training programme.

- Do they expect high standards of personal service?
- Are they looking for advice and guidance?
- Do they expect a high level of product knowledge?
- Is speed of service important?

USING TRAINING CONSULTANCIES

194

There are times when a standard training package may not be appropriate. A training consultancy will be able to develop a customised training programme. A consultancy looks closely at the business goals, the number of staff, their experience and training, and the level of customer satisfaction. In that way, training is tailored to local market conditions.

MOTIVATE YOUR STAFF

Incentive programmes are integral to staff development. Staff need to know that there are suitable rewards for building high levels of customer satisfaction as well as increasing sales.

ACTION

▶ **Have you defined the staff skills you need to improve retail performance?**

▶ **Do you have your own training resources, or do you need to use training specialists?**

▶ **Do standard training packages meet your needs or would customised training be more appropriate?**

▶ **Have you integrated incentives with your training programme?**

Improving product information

When customers come into a retail outlet, they may not intend to buy, they may simply be looking for information. But how easy is it to get information, either from staff or from product literature and display material. Helping your customers make decisions is an effective way of encouraging them to return.

MAKING A SALES AREA MORE FRIENDLY

A car manufacturer decided to open up a showroom which had no cars, but simply provided information in various forms which customers could collect and ask about. It featured interactive video, leaflet dispensers, displays and . . . no sales staff! Research showed that customers regarded the traditional car showroom as an intimidating area. They knew that they would be subjected to considerable pressure whenever they showed interest. Customers wanted to be free to browse but they also wanted to be able to get the right level of information. The publications and the interactive video provided a starting point, but, if customers wanted further information, they made the decision to approach the staff. This approach is based on a careful assessment of customer attitudes, rather than the requirements of a sales programme.

195

MAKING PRODUCT INFORMATION MORE USABLE

A retailer selling domestic electrical products found that customers were confused by the bewildering choice of products offering similar features. Suppliers' literature sets out product information in different formats so that it is not easily compared and display material simply adds to the visual confusion. The retailer works at two levels to improve the situation. He or she develops a series of standard display modules which provide essential product information. Suppliers are asked to represent their information within this format so that products can be easily compared.

HELPING CUSTOMERS MAKE THEIR OWN CHOICE

The retailer also invests in an interactive video system. This allows customers to work their way through a series of questions about a product and helps them define their own requirements. Take an audio system, for example; the questions might include:

- Do you want hi-fi quality?
- Do you want compact disc?
- Do you want separates or an integrated system?
- How powerful should the system be?
- Should it be portable?

The customer builds up a profile of requirements and the system then provides a list of suitable products and prices.

HELPING SALES STAFF PRESENT PRODUCTS

Smaller retailers who cannot afford to invest in this level of technology can train their sales staff to guide customers through the same process. By developing simple loose-leaf presenters which group products in broad bands they can help customers select the product they need.

ACTION

- ▶ **How important is product information to your customers?**
- ▶ **Can you co-operate with suppliers to achieve consistency of information?**
- ▶ **Are you able to invest in information technology to improve product information?**
- ▶ **Do you support your sales staff with product information and training?**

Focusing facilities on the customer

To distinguish itself from the competition, retail outlets should focus their operating standards on the customer. Quality and consistency in meeting customer expectations can be achieved through setting 'customer focus standards' which cover the type of training, the staffing levels, facilities, and standards of service offered to customers.

DIFFERENTIATING A RETAIL OUTLET

Research shows that retailers can differentiate their service in a number of ways: through the environment, the branding of the outlet, the quality of service offered, the clarity of the offer and the convenience. Customers want to have a consistency of service in every department; they do not distinguish between departments and any weak links will reflect on the whole organisation.

BUILDING A REPUTATION FOR SERVICE

197

The outlet's reputation for service is one of the key factors in repeat sales and customer loyalty. The retail outlet should not be a hostile environment where customers have to face over-enthusiastic staff or long queues – if customers feel comfortable and satisfied, they will return.

IMPROVING CONVENIENCE

The retail outlet should look closely at all aspects of its business where they impact on customer satisfaction. A high street retailer found that, although it was conveniently located, many of its customers were moving away from traditional shopping areas to out-of-town retail centres where it was simpler to park. Late evening opening one night a week was the choice of many shoppers while others preferred the convenience of mail order.

MOTIVATING RETAILERS TO MEET STANDARDS

Customer focus standards help retailers achieve high levels of customer satisfaction. By surveying customers' attitudes to the outlet, it is possible to measure how well individual outlets are progressing in meeting those standards. The results of the surveys can be used to set up improvement programmes and to control the levels of support retailers are given. By offering retailers higher levels of support in return for higher standards of customer satisfaction, the programmes incorporate a powerful form of motivation.

ACTION

- ▶ **Have you got a set of customer focus standards?**
- ▶ **Have you researched the factors customers look for in a retail outlet?**
- ▶ **Can you measure retailers' achievements in improving customer standards?**
- ▶ **Do you link progress in customer standards to levels of business support?**

Giving customers even greater choice

Stores with large sales areas are making greater use of the space by offering in-store concessions to other non-competitive retailers who set up specialist outlets within the store. This provides the retailer with additional rental income and makes more productive use of the sales space. It also offers their customers much greater variety and choice, plus the convenience of shopping under one roof.

MATCHING THE NEW PRODUCTS TO YOUR CUSTOMER PROFILE

The marketing team plan to introduce a carefully selected group of in-store retailers to create the right image for the store. It is important to have the right profile so that it matches the customer base and attracts new prospects who will be able to use the other facilities in the store. This broadens the customer base in a carefully planned way and can either take the store up-market or give it a more popular identity. By giving existing customers a greater choice, it helps to retain their loyalty.

INVOLVING STAFF IN THE NEW PROGRAMME

The launch has to be carefully controlled so that staff see benefits, rather than a change that threatens their own careers. Staff, for example, could be concerned about their employment prospects, sensing the arrival of other staff and wondering whether the store is in financial difficulties. The change should be explained as part of a planned programme of expansion that will attract even more customers and benefit the whole store. The recruitment of new staff should be seen as part of a programme of specialist training and development and, wherever possible, new retailers should be encouraged to take on existing staff from the store.

199

MARKETING CO-OPERATION WITH THE NEW OUTLETS

The concessions must be carefully identified within the overall store. They may carry their own identity which has been built up over a long period by branding and should not be weakened. Concessions which do their own advertising should be encouraged to include references to the main retailer. This will help to build store traffic and provide opportunities for joint promotions.

TELLING CUSTOMERS ABOUT THE CHANGE

Customer communications are important at the early stage of the launch to ensure that customers understand that there is now even greater choice at their local store. They should be aware that they are dealing with specialists and they will get an even higher standard of service. The introduction of a new concession is an opportunity for a special launch event and this can be tied in with a related promotion. Regular customers who use the services of the new concession should be rewarded with a loyalty bonus and new customers of the concession who shop in the main store can be given a special introductory offer on products from the main store.

ACTION

- ▶ **Can you broaden customer choice by co-operating with other retailers?**

- ▶ **Can you use this co-operation to strengthen your marketing and promotional activities?**

- ▶ **Can you offer your staff improved career prospects in the new operation?**

- ▶ **Does the new operation give you the opportunity to broaden your customer base?**

Retail card marketing

Card marketing is an effective way of building customer loyalty to a store. The store issues a credit or charge card for use in a defined group of retail outlets and this encourages repeat purchase. The card makes purchasing more convenient for the customers and also provides information on the customer which can be used as the basis of a direct marketing programme.

The problem that store card operators face is that they are in competition with other card operators and they may not offer the most competitive rates of interest. Conventional bank credit cards, for example, normally offer lower rates of interest and they are normally acceptable in most stores.

USING THE CARD TO MAKE SPECIAL OFFERS

The store has to offer something special over and above the normal credit card facilities to attract users and retain their loyalty. One approach is to make special offers to customers who use their charge cards on certain sale days or who purchase up to a certain value. There should also be a loyalty bonus for regular or frequent purchase so that card-holders feel they are privileged customers. As part of the in-store merchandising material, card-holders and potential holders can get leaflets which tell them about the full range of facilities they can get through their cards.

REWARDING LOYALTY

Previews of sales or other special events can be used to attract card-holders and encourage additional spending. For example, an invitation to a spring sale with an additional discount to card-holders can provide the right level of incentive. Mailing is another important loyalty builder. Customers receive monthly statements and these can be backed up by card-holder catalogues or other special offers.

EXTENDING THE USE OF THE CARD

A retailing group can add value to a store card by extending its use to other group stores. This gives the customer additional purchasing power without applying for additional finance. It also introduces the customer to the scope of the retailing group and encourages sampling of other outlets. The technology exists to integrate a home shopping service with a card marketing programme. The database information could be used to target customers with special offers and the cards could be converted to 'intelligent cards' which are linked to an electronic payments system.

OFFERING ADDITIONAL FINANCIAL SERVICES

As well as the charge and credit-card facilities, the retailer can also offer additional financial services. The retailer already holds the customer's details so it is easy to make priority offers which simplify the application process and add extra value to the loan. A number of retailers are also offering banking and cash withdrawal facilities to card-holders so that they enjoy the highest levels of convenience.

ENSURING EFFECTIVE USE OF THE CARD PROGRAMME

Any card system will fail to yield its full value if it is not used properly at store level. The head office or the card operating company is responsible for the direct marketing programmes and for maintaining an effective level of customer service and communications. They should also be building the long-term programmes which will improve levels of customer loyalty, but this can be weakened if the stores do not operate it properly. The retail marketing group sets up a programme of special promotions which can be operated at store level.

ENCOURAGING STAFF TO USE CARD-HOLDER OPPORTUNITIES

The team issue a guide to the retail activity needed to operate successful card-holder promotions. This includes timetables, the promotional support available and sample invitations. It is also important to motivate the retail staff to make the most of the card marketing opportunities. The marketing team develop an incentive programme which can be used to encourage card prospecting, event management and repeat purchase. Staff receive points for activities which contribute to the overall success of the programme and these points qualify them for special gifts and allow them to participate in a special prize draw which offers major prize opportunities.

ACTION

- ▶ **Can you develop a card payment system for your customers?**
- ▶ **Are you building a marketing programme that takes advantage of card-holder information?**
- ▶ **Can you extend the facilities available on the card to add value?**
- ▶ **Are you helping retailers take full advantage of the card?**

Building customer loyalty at the point-of-sale

There are a number of widely used promotional techniques to increase repeat purchase which can be integrated with longer-term programmes to build loyalty.

COLLECTING GIFT VOUCHERS

Gift vouchers encourage long-term purchase, regardless of competitor pricing or other forms of discounting. Customers collect the vouchers each time they make a purchase and exchange them for attractive gifts.

SELECTING THE RIGHT GIFTS

It is the quality of gift which distinguishes the offer from other low-quality promotions. Earlier forms of premium offer featuring plastic roses and cheap gifts had given sales promotion a tarnished image, but the situation has now been improved. The gifts should be of a quality which reflects the brand image of the product and encourage purchase.

203

MAKING GIFTS ACCESSIBLE

The gift programme should be structured to attract regular and occasional buyers. Lower value gifts enable a retailer to reward customers frequently and quickly, while the higher value prizes encourage customers to continue buying regularly over a long period of time.

MAKING GIFT SCHEMES EASY TO MANAGE

A gift scheme must be easy to administer – retailers do not want to get involved in complex schemes which require stockholding or lengthy administration procedures. Simple order forms and an efficient distribution system from a central location ensure that retailers can provide an efficient service to their customers.

INVOLVING RETAILERS IN THE PROMOTION

To encourage participation, retailers were rewarded with a bonus scheme based on the levels of gift redemption. The scheme also offered incentives to counter staff for offering vouchers to their customers.

ACTION

- ▸ **Can you structure a promotional scheme to encourage repeat sales?**
- ▸ **Are you rewarding occasional and regular buyers?**
- ▸ **Are your promotional schemes simple to operate?**
- ▸ **Do the programmes motivate retailers to participate?**

Summary

In the retail sector, the quality of personal service makes a major contribution to building customer satisfaction and loyalty. However, there are many other factors which can be used to retain customers. This chapter described a number of techniques, including:

- improving the quality of staff by providing training and sales support;
- improving product information so that customers find it easier to buy from you;
- focusing facilities on the customer to attract customers;
- giving customers greater choice by introducing new products and facilities;
- using card marketing to build customer information and reward loyalty; and
- building customer loyalty at the point-of-sale by using sales promotion techniques to encourage repeat purchase.

These techniques can be used by any company that sells its products through retail outlets.

18

Conclusion

Building and retaining customer loyalty is a vital issue for every organisation. As the models in Part II show, the techniques to achieve this are wide-ranging, but many of them are common to different types of business:

- providing customers with additional services;
- offering higher value than your competitors;
- increasing your customers' dependence on your business;
- offering customers the highest standards of service;
- making it easier for your customers to deal with you; and
- helping your customers improve the performance of their own business.

In many cases, the models provide ready-made examples of customer loyalty programmes which can be put into action immediately. However, to introduce programmes without considering the fundamental principles of customer loyalty or setting up an appropriate management structure is simply 'papering over the cracks'.

As Part I of the book shows, the customer loyalty process must be carefully managed to provide the optimum benefit. The key management actions are to:

- allocate responsibility to the managers and staff who will be directly involved in building customer loyalty;
- identify all opportunities to build customer loyalty by

analysing your business, your customers and your competitors' activities;

- take the initiative by making customer loyalty a priority and setting defined standards for people in your organisation to follow;

- build staff commitment and understanding by improving internal awareness of customer loyalty issues and demonstrating the individual contribution staff can make;

- raise customer awareness of your loyalty programmes by improving customer contact, consulting your customers and integrating customer loyalty messages into all your communications;

- provide your staff with the skills to make an effective contribution to customer loyalty; and

- build partnership with your key customers so that you strengthen business relationships and protect your market share.

By ensuring that your organisation is committed to building customer loyalty, you will ensure the long-term success and profitability of your business.

Index

■

added value 41–2, 74, 75, 78, 98, 100,
  152, 198
aftercare 24, 35, 159, 160
auditing customer care 52, 55

branding 111, 113

car dealership examples xiii, 158–174
communications, contribution of 23,
  24, 25, 65, 66, 73, 78, 79, 87, 88,
  91, 116, 179
community programmes 172, 173
competitive activity 13, 40, 95, 127,
  128
complaints, handling 29, 34, 37, 38,
  62, 63
components business examples xi,
  108
consultancy business examples xii
contact, importance of 10, 17, 34, 36,
  44, 61, 97–8, 133, 150, 158–9, 160,
  166–7
convenience 94–8, 109–11, 128–9,
  160, 164–5, 171, 181, 194
core skills, marketing 103–4, 136,
  149, 155
customer awareness, raising viii, 61,
  66, 125
customer consultation 62, 74
customer expectations 56–7
customer feedback 75, 98, 195
customer focus 5–6, 26, 27, 28, 31, 38,
  45, 51, 154, 183, 193
customer panels 38–9, 62
customer satisfaction 2, 25, 61, 90,
  158
customers for life 3, 11, 12, 95, 175,
  176, 177
customer reception 29, 63, 86–8
customer retention 7–8
customer relationships 10, 17, 73, 74,
  79, 81, 84, 88, 89, 90, 94, 97, 133,
  156, 167, 176, 182

direct marketing 62, 64–5, 133, 134
distribution 118–20
distributor development 121–3,
  128–31, 158–74

financial institutions examples xiv,
  11, 175–89
fleet business 168–71

importance v, 2–15
information systems business
  examples xiii, 36, 150–7
incentive programmes 17, 58–60, 73,
  191, 194
initiatives, taking 45–50

leadership commitment 45–6
life cycle analysis 42–4, 74, 136–7
long-term business performance 3–4,
  13

management services 104–7, 111,
  114, 138–9, 144–6, 169, 171, 183,
  184–5, 187–8
management training 69

oil industry examples xi, 100, 107
opportunities, identifying vii, 34–44
ownership cycle 2
ownership experience 9–10
own-label development 113–15

partnership 14, 21, 44, 71–7, 78, 85,
  90, 121, 143, 148, 186
planned maintenance 82–4
product development 4–5, 22–3
product information 192–3
purchase cycles 8–9, 72

quality, importance of 2, 4, 19, 21, 22,
     26, 35, 46, 47, 52, 68, 78, 80, 81,
     85, 90, 117–18, 125

repeat purchase 6–7, 8, 11, 13
research, customer 4–5, 9, 38–40, 46,
     131, 154
research and development,
     contract 22, 62, 100, 101
responsibility, allocating vi, 16–33,
     45, 49, 55, 68
     sales 17–18
     distribution 18–19
     manufacturing 20–21
     purchasing 21–22
     design and development 22–23
     marketing 23–24
     communications 25
     personnel 26–27
     training 27–28
     customer service 28–29
     administration 29–30
     quality 31
     service 32–33
retail concessions 195–7
retail examples xiv, 190–201

sales force 12, 54
satisfaction surveys 4, 39, 63
services, contribution of x, 11, 32, 35,
     74, 78–99, 108–9, 141, 151
service business examples 78–99
service levels 91–4, 95–7, 156, 177–8,
     185
service packages 79–80, 92, 110, 180
service, single source 79–82
special offers 7, 161, 162, 197, 200
staff commitment, building viii, 51,
     60, 176, 181
staff skills, developing ix, 67–70, 122,
     150, 152, 155, 190
statement of direction 48

technical support 100, 102–3, 109,
     110, 120–1, 153, 169
total business solutions 36–7, 136,
     138, 141, 146, 148, 150
training 4, 19, 26, 41, 51, 61, 67, 68–9,
     122, 124, 141, 155, 163, 190–1
travel industry examples xii, 124–35

value engineering 115–20